"It's been nearly a century since Albert 'Ginger' Goodwin was shot and killed in the Cumberland bush on Canada's Vancouver Island, but thanks to people such as playwright Elaine Ávila, the legacy of the workers' rights activist won't soon be forgotten." —*CASCADIA WEEKLY*

"It's a story as familiar to people in the US as in Canada – a large corporation comes to a town where they want to develop or deliver resources and they promise work and money, a boom, if the citizens will let the corporation have its way." —*NATIONAL OBSERVER*

"Elaine Ávila's plays reflect how deeply she cares about the world and about us. Whether in the recent or more distant past, she connects us to the brave souls who take a human stand against the forces of oppression. Telling the stories of immigrants and working people, she is not afraid to show the human toll of pollution and overwork on love and family. But she also shows how they fight to preserve the roots of their music, cuisine, and language ... These are plays that reach out to us, reminding us how much we share, how much we have to lose, and how much we have to give." —OLIVER MAYER, playwright and director of MFA Dramatic Writing Program, USC School of Dramatic Arts

"The two plays in this volume centre on workers' rights, the conditions and effects of labour on people's bodies and on the lands they inhabit, and how standing up for rights in the workplace benefit communities at large. Centring and celebrating interdependence rather than dogmatic neoliberal independence are key to cherishing these plays. Enjoy Ávila's vision for a better world, finely tuned and crafted, heartfelt and real." —CARIDAD SVICH, Obie Award for Lifetime Acheivement, author of *Twelve Ophelias*

"[*Kitimat* is] a beautiful piece about having a voice, expressed through mothers, sisters, and daughters, and ending with such power and simplicity, as to have the past sing to the future. Really lovely." —LUIS ALFARO, author of *Mojada* and MacArthur Fellow

ALSO BY ELAINE ÁVILA

PLAYS

*Fado: The Saddest Music in the World**
Jane Austen, Action Figure and Other Plays

PLAYS IN ANTHOLOGIES

Lighting the Way: An Anthology of Short Plays about the Climate Crisis
(edited by Chantal Bilodeau)
*Monologues for Latino/a Actors: A Resource Guide to Contemporary
Latino/a Playwrights for Actors and Teachers* (edited by Micha Espinosa)
Scenes for Latinx Actors: Voices of the New American Theatre (edited by
Cynthia DeCure and Micha Espinosa)
24 Gun Control Plays (edited by Caridad Svich and Zac Kline)
Where Is the Hope? An Anthology of Short Climate Change Theatre Plays
(edited by Chantal Bilodeau)

ESSAYS IN ANTHOLOGIES

Antologia literária Satúrnia: Autores luso-canadianos
(edited by Manuel Carvalho)
Casting a Movement: The Welcome Table Initiative
(edited by Claire Syler and Daniel Banks)
Innovations in Five Acts: Strategies for Theatre and Performance
(edited by Caridad Svich)
Into the Azorean Sea: Bilingual Anthology of Azorean Poetry
(edited by Diniz Borges)
Stages of Resistance: Theatre and Politics in the Capitalocene
(edited by Caridad Svich with Olivia George)

*Published by Talonbooks

THE BALLAD OF GINGER GOODWIN

&

KITIMAT

TWO PLAYS FOR WORKERS

by Elaine Ávila

with forewords by

Kathleen Flaherty & Rosa Simas

and a preface by the author

TALONBOOKS

Talonbooks
9259 Shaughnessy Street, Vancouver, British Columbia, Canada v6p 6r4
talonbooks.com

Talonbooks is located on xʷməθkʷəy̓əm, Sḵwx̱wú7mesh, and səlilwətaɬ Lands.

First printing: 2023

Typeset in Minion
Printed and bound in Canada on 100% post-consumer recycled paper

Cover and interior design by Typesmith
Cover image by Typesmith

Talonbooks acknowledges the financial support of the Canada Council for
the Arts, the Government of Canada through the Canada Book Fund, and the
Province of British Columbia through the British Columbia Arts Council and the
Book Publishing Tax Credit.

Rights to produce *The Ballad of Ginger Goodwin & Kitimat: Two Plays for
Workers*, in whole or in part, in any medium by any group, amateur or
professional, are retained by the author. Interested persons are requested to
contact the author care of Talonbooks.

Library and Archives Canada Cataloguing in Publication

Title: The ballad of Ginger Goodwin & Kitimat : two plays for workers / by Elaine
Ávila ; with forewords by Kathleen Flaherty and Rosa Simas and a preface by the
author.
Other titles: Plays. Selections | Kitimat
Names: Ávila, Elaine, 1965- author. | Container of (work): Ávila, Elaine,
1965- Kitimat.
Description: Includes bibliographical references.
Identifiers: Canadiana 2023043987X | ISBN 9781772014471 (softcover)
Subjects: LCSH: Goodwin, Ginger—Drama. | LCSH: Kitimat-Stikine
(B.C.)—Drama.
Classification: LCC PS8551.V535 A6 2023 | DDC C812/.6—dc23

vii   **PREFACE** by Elaine Ávila

THE BALLAD OF GINGER GOODWIN

1   The Ballad of Ginger Goodwin

3   Foreword by Kathleen Flaherty

6   Production History

7   Cast

8   Setting & Time

71   Acknowledgments

KITIMAT

73   Kitimat

75   Foreword by Rosa Simas:
From the Azores to the Anthropocene

80   Production History

81   Cast

82   Time, Place, Setting & Playwright's Note

156   Acknowledgments

APPENDICES

157   Statements from Directors about the Premiere
Productions

159   Further Reading, Listening, and Viewing

PREFACE by Elaine Ávila

Before I wrote these plays, I was naive. I believed theatre leaders who claimed that the exclusion of stories by women, workers, immigrants, refugees, IBPOC folks, and LGBTQIA2S+ folks from our stages was an oversight of some kind. I believed that North American theatre was a well-intentioned project in which, eventually, people of all classes, genders, races, and cultures would be included.

The source of my naivety was complex. Before I immigrated to this place called Canada, I grew up on the unceded Lands of the Ohlone now known as Silicon Valley. The place cultivated its own extreme brand of optimism: the belief that brainchildren would make you rich, that there were no limits to anything (especially to what you could invent and sell), and that worrying about the climate crisis was needless because we could invent space shields and robot bees. It seemed true. As I grew up, Facebook started as a dating app. Google paved asphalt over orchards (as if we could eat search engines). We didn't speak of the workers who made these inventions, or of the mining involved in making them. We didn't speak of reciprocity or of taking only what we needed. But there were inventions in social justice, too. I grew up in one of the first racially integrated neighbourhoods in the United States, now known as the Third Willow Glen Eichler Development. Now the homes are considered collectible and they are a tourist attraction, complete with drive-by tours. This development was a suburb designed by postwar real-estate developer Joseph Eichler and a social experiment mentioned by James Baldwin in the 1963 Richard O. Moore documentary *Take This Hammer*.[1] I was bussed into a public performing-arts high school as a white kid, another social experiment, which meant most of the students I went to school with were queer, "unwed" mothers, Vietnamese, and/or Latinx. For me this wasn't unusual, to be in a racially and socially mixed place; it was simply life.

Meanwhile, I didn't understand that my whiteness was rather precarious. On my father's side, I was Azorean Portuguese, but I grew up outside the community and didn't speak the language: I was "assimilated." I didn't know how the deportation of Latinx Peoples may have led to the way we vehemently embraced being "American." As for my mother, she had been adopted – yet another social experiment – and all traces of her birth lineage had been wiped out as an attempt to graft her onto her racially similar, alternate set of parents. As far as I knew, we were legitimate middle class. I had no idea that being so came at the cost of making our family

---

1   Watch it online on the Bay Area Television Archive (part of the J. Paul Leonard Library's Department of Special Collections), diva.sfsu.edu/collections/sfbatv/bundles/187041.

histories invisible. We never spoke of our peasant past. Instead, my father worked for NASA, so we dreamed of the inventions we would need for space, both practical, like having to eat food engineered from algae, and social, such as *Star Trek* creator Gene Rodenberry's dream of abolishing currencies, meeting all human needs, and pursuing our passions without compensation. I found it exciting. I wrote stories about rockets and finding other civilizations on other planets.

When I married my trumpet-player husband and immigrated to the unceded Traditional Territories of the xʷməθkʷəy̓əm (Musqueam), Sḵwx̱wú7mesh (Squamish), and səlilwətaɬ (Tsleil-Waututh) Nations, or "Vancouver," proudly becoming a "Canadian citizen," and part of his working-class family, I began to understand that there are certain stories we aren't told, and for a reason. I learned about Ginger Goodwin and how "Canada" got the eight-hour day from my father-in-law, Bill Clark Sr., a nationally prominent labour leader (he was constantly on the news, commemorated in books, once made the cover of *Maclean's* Magazine, and was untiringly passionate about social justice). Then I learned that almost no one in "Canada" learned this history in school. I learned there had been multiple attempts to create plays about Ginger Goodwin, but they had all collapsed for one reason or another. Signs commemorating Goodwin were taken down by right-wing governments. Not long after Ginger Goodwin was assassinated on July 27, 1918, the *Vancouver Daily Sun* wrote, "Let his friends grieve if they will, but let all other good citizens cease to mention him henceforth."[2] Good citizens? Would that mean that every person who would want to remember this history could be labelled as "evil"? That their citizenship might be in question? Yes, it could. I was frequently told I "better be careful" while working on the play. Was it a threat? Yes, it was. Perhaps to give myself courage, I wanted to know the songs Ginger Goodwin and his friends had sung, to learn them, and to incorporate them in the play.

When I asked my father-in-law how scared he thought Ginger Goodwin might have been before he went to hide in the bush, whether or not he was aware he might be killed, Bill Sr. shared his own history in leading strikes. He told me how he'd personally received so many death threats during a strike he had led that he had collapsed on the street with a heart attack. So yes, Ginger knew, and he was probably terrified. As Bill Sr. said, "I had a heart attack, didn't I?" But both Ginger Goodwin and Bill Sr. persevered, stood up. And I learned that plenty of stories are censored or suppressed, even now, within our North American democracies, because they have great power.

---

2 "German or British – Which?," *Vancouver Daily Sun*, August 2, 1918, 1, vancouver sun.newspapers.com/clip/122635173/.

When I was asked to write an environmental play by Prof. Art Horowitz and Prof. James Taylor at Pomona College, I was emboldened. (Both men recently passed away; may they rest in peace.) I decided to centre the play on Kitimat, known as the "fastest declining town in Canada." When I started the play, Kitimat was rapidly becoming known as the only municipality in North America to organize a vote on whether or not they wanted a Big Oil pipeline to come to their town. Former Kitimat residents, now living in the Lower Mainland or in Los Angeles, predicted that current residents would choose to embrace the promise of a big industrial project with the potential to raise Kitimat's property values. I also knew it was likely that residents would speak to me about what they were going through, because Kitimat used to be 40 percent Portuguese, mostly Azoreans. This was my cultural background, and I'd been embracing it, learning my ancestral language and history as part of a project to decolonize, to unassimilate.

While researching the play, I volunteered at the Luso Canadian Hall in Kitimat, cooking all day with the women in the community. The men got wind that I was a writer and joined us in the kitchen, regaling us with stories of the medieval plays they'd put on – in Portuguese – in the hall. When you start swapping stories, you're going to find some treasures. An eighty-year-old Azorean woman, chopping carrots with me, a refugee from the 1957–1958 Capelinhos volcanic explosion on the island of Faial, and one of the first female immigrants to Kitimat, taught me to speak Portuguese with the Faialense accent of my grandmother, who died when I was young. Another eighty-year-old woman, from the Azorean Island of São Miguel, sang a fado song she'd written, then began singing "Sapateia" to me, the first song I'd heard from my ancestral lands. Turns out it contains many suppressed, inspiring, and magical histories.

"Sapateia," like many Portuguese words, is highly resonant, full of meanings. Here are a few of my favourite definitions:

the snare of immigration;
a call to action;
the sound dancers' shoes make when tap dancing; and
the art of dance itself, with connections to the zapateo of
Argentinian gauchos and the footwork of flamenco.

The woman who first sang "Sapateia" to me confided that it is about a young woman who rebels against her father's wishes by falling in love with the village shoemaker. Esteemed authors and Portuguese literary scholars Dr. Onésimo Almeida and Dr. Francisco Fagundes shared that "Sapateia" is known both as a song and a dance, with many versions in existence, one of the most famous being from São Miguel. As Dr. Almeida wrote to me in personal correspondence, "the lyrics invite people to dance in spite of the hardships of life." "Sapateia" protests poverty. Also in personal correspondence, Dr. Fagundes wrote to me: "The semantic import of the song's refrain is, 'Let's tap dance, let's tap dance,' for what else can we do in a place where lunch is both lunch and dinner, that is: 'We are all starving to death, so let's tap dance.'" For me, this song says it all. The Portuguese dictatorship, the longest in modern times, left people starving and without access to education, which is why so many of our families had to immigrate.

So many stories we Azorean immigrants inherit are about shoes. The accomplished actor Paul Moniz de Sá tells me his uncle walked across the island of São Miguel barefoot, shoes in hand, to court his future wife. Paul's uncle only put his shoes on when he reached her window. It sounds like a fairy tale, but it contains some harsh economic realities: shoes were expensive. It was more important at the time to protect them (and the potential they had to change your life) than to protect your feet. Shoes, if you could get them, helped their wearers transcend class barriers. In fascist Portugal, you needed shoes to go to the city; those too poor for a pair would search a pile of discarded shoes, selecting the ill-matched and the ill-fitting for a chance at a better life. My cousin Lina Ávila told me that Azorean immigrants developed "expensive tastes for shoes and refrigerators," which ended up inspiring a whole storyline in *Kitimat*, which forms the second part of this book. No wonder a young woman falls in love with her shoemaker: he's giving her wings to fly, agency to dance.

Recently, my friend the fadista Sara Marreiros let me try on a pair of shoes that her uncle Antonio Marreiros, a sapateiro (shoemaker) from the small village of Hortas do Tabual, had made for her when she was eighteen. Magically, they still fit. Antonio had planned ahead: he hadn't used modern shoe sizes but had drawn an outline of the shape of Sara's feet. Sara encouraged me to slip them on, so I could learn from the inside, from sentido, from tactility. I felt how the shoe framed my heel, lifted my arch. The leather had been shaped by hand, crafted to cradle and boost. They were wings, made specifically for my friend. Discussing her uncle the sapateiro, Sara and I spoke about how fascist deprivation during the Estado Novo years meant we were only one generation away from older ways of living, without electricity and running water, ways of living sustainably and making things by hand. We shared stories about going backwards to our shared past and how this could help us move forward. It brings tears to my eyes to think that I might have lost all of this because I didn't know how much it mattered.

When a resident of Kitimat heard about the Los Angeles premiere of the play on a Kitimat Facebook group, he posted this response: "This proves that everyone's story matters, no matter how small, or out of the way." *Exactly.*

Thomas King finishes each story in his 2003 CBC Massey Lecture, "The Truth about Stories: A Native Narrative," with the following:

> It's yours [this story]. Do with it what you will. Tell it to friends. Turn it into a television movie. Forget it. *But don't say in the years to come that you would have lived your life differently if only you had heard this story.* You've heard it now.[3]

The two plays in this book have made it possible for me, and others, to live our lives differently. When *The Ballad of Ginger Goodwin* was first produced, on the unceded, Traditional, and Ancestral Territories of the Noxws'áʔaq (Nooksack), SEMYOME (Semiahmoo), Xws7ámesh (Samish), and Lhaq'temish (Lummi) Nations at Western Washington University in Bellingham, Washington, Kathleen Weiss, director and long-time collaborator, noticed the unique dedication among the student actors to the story. This was because the lands there had the same geology, the same mining and labour histories as could be found when and where Ginger Goodwin lived. The students' family stories were becoming less invisibilized. One actor and his father came to me after the play, with tears in their eyes, and shared their own history with hard labour – a moment I will forever treasure. They said that their access to university degrees had come from backbreaking work. In my own family, my Azorean grandfather literally broke many ribs while hauling giant tuna out of the sea so his son and daughter could go to university (when he could not). When the parents of director Janet Hayatshashi came to the premiere of *Kitimat*, they too shared stories of how Big Oil had impacted their lives, forcing them to immigrate. Considering these stories, learning about these histories, sharing and swapping them, has inspired connection. It has awakened gratitude, pride, and courage and a different kind of idealism for the future. While I will always dream of outer space, I also know we can stand together on this planet to face what comes.

I hope you enjoy and thank you for reading.

—ELAINE ÁVILA

> Unceded, Ancestral, and Traditional Territories of the qiqéyt (Qayqayt) First Nation and other Coast Salish Peoples (New Westminster, British Columbia) March 2023

---

3 Thomas King, "'You'll Never Believe What Happened' Is Always a Great Way to Start," in *The Truth about Stories: A Native Narrative*, CBC Massey Lectures (Toronto: House of Anansi, 2003), 29. Emphasis mine.

Bill Clark Sr., president of the Telecommunications Workers Union (TWU), during the major, lengthy, and pivotal strike of 1980–1981, as he prepares to speak to the press.

Photo: Sean Griffin, Pacific Tribune Photograph Collection, SFU

THE BALLAD OF GINGER GOODWIN

For workers

and

for Bill Clark Sr., former president of Telecommunications
Workers Union, and his wife, Gwen Clark

FOREWORD by Kathleen Flaherty

> I want freedom, the right to self-expression, everybody's right
> to beautiful, radiant things.
>
> —**EMMA GOLDMAN**
> *Living My Life* (1931)

Elaine Ávila, cheerfully, vibrantly, energetically, purposefully, makes theatre
as if it were a political act. When she asks you to come along on her journey
of development, she is initiating you into an ever-growing company of artists
involved in political action.

Elaine began this play, *The Ballad of Ginger Goodwin*, as a tribute to her late
father-in-law, the labour activist Bill Clark Sr. It brought Ginger Goodwin to life
for me and for others as she created it; together, we became part of his story,
part of our collective stories of labour struggles. Surely, that's the reason we
love art – it provides joy in discovery of ourselves and in revelation of truths
we can carry with us.

When she first proposed the play, Elaine was incensed that people, even in
the places Ginger Goodwin had lived and worked, had no idea of his life and
work – a life that seemed to be *about* work, tireless work that culminated in
the adoption of the eight-hour work day. Even worse, people had actively suppressed memory of him. Interviewed about the play in early 2016 by *Cascadia
Weekly*, Elaine had said:

> Goodwin's assassination led to Vancouver's first general strike,
> to Canada's first general strike. It seems like pretty important his-
> tory, right? But after he was assassinated, the *Vancouver [Daily]
> Sun* newspaper wrote, "Let his friends grieve if they will, but let
> all other good citizens cease to mention him henceforth." In the
> years since his death, people have been fighting to keep his story
> out of the public eye.[4]

Surely that's enough provocation for any curious person to dig a little deeper.

It's difficult to work with a playwright unless you can keep up with the conversation, and Elaine and I share a love of research. She can retain the details
better than me, but it wasn't long before I was able to recite certain facts, including Ginger's Yorkshire beginnings, his legendary battles for workers' rights, his
speeches, and his violent death in Cumberland, BC. The cover-up, the active
suppression of his memory, is curious in itself. Clearly, there are lots of potential

---

4   From Amy Kepferle, "Ginger's Ballad: Workers of the World, Unite!," *Cascadia Weekly*
    11, no. 5 (February 3, 2016): 16, washingtondigitalnewspapers.org/?a=is&oid=CASWEEK
    LY20160203.1.16&type=staticpdf. The *Vancouver Daily Sun*'s quote was corrected for
    accuracy (see the preface, note 2).

stories around Ginger Goodwin, but Elaine focused on the last campaign in Trail, BC, before his death and took him to his last breath. This added the complexities of patriotism and war profiteering to the fight for workers' rights.

When Elaine creates a play, she uses the clay of real life to shape the large trajectory and the small moments. Most details of what she discovers remain as ghosts, whispering through the final production – a word, a phrase, the colour of a ribbon – but they anchor the piece in authenticity. Sometimes what she uncovers becomes the beating heart of the play; always, it provides texture. Where to go in service of these curiosities is a combination of diligence, rigour, and kismet – one source leads to another, to another, deeper, closer to the story. Elaine was researching the music of the miners from Ginger's childhood and later union work; I happened to know Gary Cristall, who lives at the intersection of folk music and union organizing. In their first lively meeting, Gary extrapolated from the folk music he knew that the striking miners in Trail were likely hearing what the Yorkshire miners of Ginger's youth had been singing, and promised to do more research in that direction. What I took away from that meeting, besides a dizzying array of music references, was a deeper understanding of how Elaine works: her never-ending research, and how rooted that research is in experience – meeting the people, seeing their landscape, hearing their words.

Months later, in February 2016, I was in a car with Elaine and two others on our way to Bellingham, Washington, to see a performance of *The Ballad of Ginger Goodwin* by students of Western Washington University. Some of the student performers, and perhaps some of the audience, focused on the love story that Elaine had spun to thread the political story together with the private character she extrapolated for Ginger. For those of us with potent union allegiances or even an interest in labour history, the story of the triumphant losses by the workers, of their struggle against the lure of war profiteering, was the draw. The thrill of the power of art really ran down my back, though, when Elaine told us of the students discovering their own heritage in the play. The land of the area is replete with abandoned underground mines and soaked in the sweat and blood of miners; these students could identify their own grandparents and great-grandparents as the youth lost to a cruel industry. The power of Ginger's speeches was informed by their newly discovered passion for ancestors not much older than them, fighting a battle they could not win.

The Ballad of Ginger Goodwin really came to life for me a few months later, when Elaine was invited to present excerpts of the play at a May Day celebration in Cumberland – short steps from the woods where Ginger Goodwin was murdered. It seemed foolish to direct a bunch of Vancouver actors in this endeavour, so we arranged for the late Gerri Hemphill, who was working with actors from Nanaimo, to cast and rehearse the performance of a script I cobbled together from excerpts. Elaine and I arranged to travel to Nanaimo, meet up with Gerri, and go to the performance together on the sunny Sunday afternoon of May 1, 2016. At the last minute, Elaine missed the ferry because of a traffic stall near her home in New Westminster and decided that she would feel even worse if she caught the next ferry and drove for an hour only to miss the performance. As it turned out, the car she was driving barely made it home and was never driven again.

So Elaine missed a great moment in the history of her play. She thanked the pragmatic spirit of Ginger Goodwin that her car hadn't died on Highway 19, stranding her on Vancouver Island. That's Elaine all over – a comrade who knows how to make lemonade.

One of the great joys of art in activism is the potential for buoying and juicing the fight for the cause. "Preaching to the choir," it's sometimes called. Or "entertaining the troops." These words are often spoken as if such acts weren't vital. But the fights for workers' rights continue to this day, often without fanfare. To be invited to read or perform segments of *The Ballad of Ginger Goodwin* at Cumberland's annual International Workers Day Community Bean Supper on May Day felt like a gift. The organizers who plan and execute the annual event know as much or more about Ginger Goodwin's story than we did. Their connections to the miners who had toiled in the miles of tunnels beneath us were connections of blood, sweat, and passion. So it was especially sweet to know that the proceeds from that day's bean supper were going to striking steelworkers, many of whom were present in the hall. And it was especially galvanizing for the actors to feel responsibility for the expression of Elaine's and Ginger's words for an audience thirsty for the juice – to know that the chorus of "Solidarity Forever" would feed these workers, this audience, would keep the struggle alive. There are times when activist artists educate their audience, and joyful times when they edify and recharge them. *Ginger* has done its work already. As a play it acts on players and audiences with a homegrown story of heroism and sacrifice that tenderly raises the consciousness of our history. Elaine speaks for every activist artist in *The Ballad of Ginger Goodwin*:

GINGER: I hope to be remembered –
JOE: Aye –
GINGER: When things get terribly tough –
JOE: Like they are now –
GINGER: When it all seems hopeless.
JOE: Why on earth do you want to be remembered in a terrible time?
GINGER: Because that's when it matters most. I want to be remembered
    when a worker reaches out to help a fellow worker.
JOE: Aye.
GINGER: When a worker says, "We're in this together, we can do better."[5]

   —KATHLEEN FLAHERTY
    April 2021

---

5 From act two, scene fourteen.

PRODUCTION HISTORY

The Ballad of Ginger Goodwin was commissioned by the Western Washington University's Department of Theatre and Dance at the College of Fine and Performing Arts and first produced at the Douglas Underground Theater (DUG) of Western Washington University's Performing Arts Centre in Bellingham, Washington, from February 4 to 13, 2016, with the following cast and crew:

GINGER Goodwin – Bailey Ellis
ANNA Petroni – Marlena McHenry
JOE Naylor – Garrett Lander
MARY ANN Goodwin – Nan Tilghman
WALTER Goodwin – Aaron Ussery
LUIGI Petroni – Ryan Darian Moghadam
SELWYN Blaylock – Samuel Orrey
STEPHEN, MEDICAL EXAMINER – Peter Moleske
AL – Kyle Stella
FRANCES – Alyssa Balogh
ELSIE – Tess Nakaishi
RITA – Siara Woods-Lindholm

Producer and Department Chair – Beth Leonard
Director – Kathleen Weiss
Assistant Director – Eric Brake
Stage Manager – Griffin Harwood
Lighting Designer – Darren McCroom
Assistant Lighting Designer – Megan Birdsong
Scenic Designer – Zack Pierson
Technical Director – Christopher Bowe
Costume Designer – Mason Fraker
Costume Shop Manager – Rachel Anderson
Properties Designer – Becca Morgan
Sound Designer – Joshua Blaisdell
Shop Forman – Lucas McVey
Music Director – Ashley VanCurler
Music Consultant – Gary Cristall
Faculty Mentors – Monica Hart (Costume Design) and
    Dipu Gupta (Scenic Design)
Original Ballad "We Cannot Mend Our Ways" by Earle Peach

CAST

NOTE: Actors of all ages and ethnicities may be cast.

GINGER Goodwin, thirty-one, a smelter worker from Treeton, South Yorkshire, England

ANNA Petroni, twenty, a laundress from Calabria, Italy

JOE Naylor, forty-six, a coal miner and union organizer from Sheffield, South Yorkshire, England, and Ginger's best friend

MARY ANN Goodwin, in her fifties, Ginger's mom, also from Treeton

WALTER Goodwin, in his fifties, Ginger's dad and a coal miner, also from Treeton

LUIGI Petroni, twenty-three, Anna's brother

SELWYN Blaylock, thirty-nine, assistant manager and smelter

MEDICAL EXAMINER, in his thirties, from Nelson, British Columbia

STEPHEN, in his thirties, a federal fair-wage officer from Ottawa

AL, in his thirties, representative of the International Union of Mine, Mill, and Smelter Workers, from Denver, Colorado

FRANCES, in her forties, a pro-war matron

ELSIE, twenty-three, a chorus girl

RITA, twenty, a nurse

Smelter WORKERS

NOTE on casting, unless a larger cast is desired:

male actor 1 plays SELWYN, MEDICAL EXAMINER, STEPHEN, AL, and WORKER;

male actor 2 plays JOE, WALTER, LUIGI, and WORKER; and

female actor 3 plays FRANCES, RITA, ELSIE, MARY ANN, and WORKER.

Most characters in this play are immigrants. Therefore, GINGER, JOE, MARY ANN, and WALTER have Yorkshire accents; LUIGI and RITA have Italian accents; AL is American; SELWYN, STEPHEN, FRANCES, ELSIE, and the MEDICAL EXAMINER are Canadian-born; and the WORKERS are a mix of all of the above.

SETTING

The back porch of the Meakin Hotel in Trail, British Columbia

NOTE: Like memories or dreams, additional settings and times in the play have a fluid feeling to them and are either minimalistic or imaginary: the Union Hall, dreams, memories, the home of Selwyn Blaylock, the banks of the Columbia River, a coal seam, back home in Yorkshire, Anna's childhood home, a boardwalk, the street, a hospital, a medical office, and the woods near Cumberland, BC.

TIME

November 1917 to July 1918

NOTE: In the original production, the downstage stage area was open, and laundry tubs, benches, and bed sheets established the Meakin Hotel's back porch. For Selwyn Blaylock's home, there was a second level at the back of the stage, with a small breakfast table, above the action of the play. Below Selwyn's home, supports were visible, constructed with open slats and birch-tree pillars, suggestive of forests and a union hall. Sometimes Anna would string a load of laundry from pillar to pillar. For the hospital, a bench was used to suggest visitor seating; for the scenes with Al, a wooden negotiating table was brought onstage. For the river, a piece of cloth curling around the front of the stage suggested the banks and currents.

Anna (Marlene McHenry) and Ginger Goodwin (Bailey Ellis) dare to dream of a better day for workers, when they can love freely and build a life together.
Photo: Chris Bowe, courtesy of Western Washington University Department of Theatre Arts

Ginger Goodwin (Bailey Ellis) rallies the spirits of the workers (Garrett Lander, Nan Tilghman, Peter Moleske, Alyssa Balogh, Siara Woods-Lindhom, Tess Nakaishi, and Aaron Ussery) during the difficulties of the 1917–1918 smelter strike in Trail, BC.
Photo: Chris Bowe, courtesy of Western Washington University Department of Theatre Arts

Ginger Goodwin (Bailey Ellis) looks on compassionately as Anna (Marlene McHenry) reckons with how her cherished brother Luigi (Ryan Darian Moghadam) has lost his sight in the trenches of WW I and requires tending by his nurse, Rita (Siara Woods-Lindholm).
Photo: Chris Bowe, courtesy of Western Washington University Department of Theatre Arts

PRELUDE

*We hear a bit of a song, as if tuning into another time,
or reviving a story found deep in the earth.*

WORKER: (*singing from "The Day They Shot Ginger Down" by Gordon
Carter[6]*) It was a black day for Cumberland, a black day for
the miners ...
The day they shot Ginger down.

ALL actors enter and begin doing hard labour of various types.

---

6 On Gordon Carter's *Rivers and Roads* (2012); see gordoncarter.bandcamp.com/album/
   rivers-and-roads.

ACT ONE – Scene One
STRIKE!

November 1917. Union Hall in Trail, British Columbia.

GINGER gathers his courage and steps up to address the crowd of smelter WORKERS. He reaches out his arms awkwardly in a welcoming embrace, then drops them to his side and launches into his speech. (Note: The WORKERS' lines are divided among the cast and may be adapted to fit the number of actors available.)

GINGER: My brothers, my sisters, a new day is coming. We shall no longer know the galling chains of wage slavery with its evil effects of misery and want, insanity and crime. We shall know happiness and joy, peace and plenty. If we persevere, we shall have a piece of the profits we earn for the company.

WORKER 1: We earn their profits?

GINGER: Think of it, if we all stop working, will there be any profits for them?

WORKER 1: (*laughing*) No.

GINGER: They say the working class is lazy, but they are the ones that are idle. Flaunting their wealth before us, with their mansions on the hill.

WORKER 2: Far from the poisons we work in.

GINGER: With their monkey dinners and their blackbird pies.

WORKER 3: Far better than we eat.

GINGER: With their weekends in the country and their fancy clothes.

WORKER 4: While we're down here with the muck and the flies.

GINGER: While they profit off the death of our brothers.

WORKER 5: What's he mean?

WORKER 6: Means we make zinc. For bullets.

WORKER 5: Right.

GINGER: While our brothers die in the trenches of their war, who makes big profits?

WORKER 7: Our bosses.

WORKER 8: My brother's over there. I want him to have bullets.

WORKER 9: I do too.

WORKER 8: We shouldn't strike during wartime.

GINGER: Then they should treat us decently during wartime. Have they been reasonable? Have they been decent?

WORKERS: No.

GINGER: How do they honour their agreements? Does Mr. Blaylock honour the eight-hour day?

WORKERS: No.

GINGER: Oh. Wait. Forgive me. He *is* honouring the eight-hour day: by working you for thirteen hours and only paying you for eight.

  WORKERS boo.

WORKER 3: He drives us all hours. Building his bigger, fancier smelter.

WORKER 5: To make even more bullets.

WORKER 8: I'm afraid he'll fire me if I object.

GINGER: Is working those sorts of hours safe for you?

WORKER 8: Nothing about being down there is safe.

WORKER 1: A whole balcony collapsed on my friend.

WORKER 2: He's dead because they couldn't be bothered to check the ropes.

WORKER 3: Plus being leaded.

WORKER 4: Lead can twist your guts up at any time, anywhere.

GINGER: It's a shame when the workingman has to see to his own safety and the safety of the plant. You would think these things were basic decency. But they are not.

WORKER 5: We've got to fight for better conditions.

WORKER 6: And better hours.

WORKER 8: Mr. Blaylock says we shouldn't strike.

GINGER: They always say we can't strike. But if you take that away from us, what do we have to bargain with?

WORKER 9: Not much.

WORKER 8: What if he blacklists us?

GINGER: I've been blacklisted, my friends. It's no easy thing. I know many of you have families. That's why we have to talk this thing through. My brothers, make no mistake, these capitalists are parasites who are accustomed to living on your blood, the blood of the working class. These capitalists own the machinery of production. They own the machinery of war. These capitalists know that a strike is your power and your lever to overthrow their carelessness and their cruelty. And they will fight to keep you ignorant of your power and unable to use it.

WORKER 1: We should down tools.

WORKER 2: What if he gets the government to send in troops?

GINGER: He could do it.

WORKER 6: How will I survive without pay?

GINGER: The American branch of our union, in a great and key act of solidarity is backing us. We'll have strike pay.

WORKERS cheer.

WORKER 7: How much experience you got leading strikes?

GINGER: I've been in strikes my whole life. But this will be the first one I've led.

WORKER 8: You seem young. Do you know what you're doing? Does he know?

WORKER 9: Ginger Goodwin saved my life. I caught fire at the smelter. I was on fire. Water didn't work. It was a chemical fire. There was nothing to put it out. Ginger took his coat, threw it on me. When that wasn't enough, he threw himself on me. Risked his life to save mine. Wouldn't hardly even let me thank him.

GINGER: An injury to one is an injury to all.

WORKER 6: True.

GINGER: I believe if we strike that we will get immediate attention. We will not be ignored. Why? Because they desperately need our work for their war.

WORKER 3: Let's put it to a vote!

GINGER: Very well. My brothers, how many of you vote to strike?

Some WORKERS raise their hands to vote, others write on slips and put them in a ballot box. GINGER counts.

GINGER: (*finishing the count*) Brothers, we strike tomorrow.

A cheer, then GINGER and WORKERS sing and disperse. The song is the chorus of Joe Hill's 1913 "We Will Sing One Song" (set to the tune of Stephen Foster's 1853 "My Old Kentucky Home, Good-Night!").

ALL: (*singing*) Organize! Oh, toilers, come organize your might;
Then we'll sing one song of the workers' commonwealth,
Full of beauty, full of love and health.

ACT ONE – Scene Two

GINGER WATER

Later that night. The rickety back porch of the working-class Meakin Hotel is cluttered with wooden benches, steel tubs of water, a washboard, and a mangler. At one end of this circuit is a pile of dirty laundry; at the other, a neat stack of packages of clean clothes, wrapped in newspaper and twine.

An exhausted laundress, ANNA Petroni, is scrubbing sheets and men's clothes on the washboard. Wisps of sweaty hair curl around her face; she ties her hair back with a red ribbon. ANNA is humming a folk song from her hometown of Calabria, in southern Italy; it's perhaps a Calabrian tarantella, or a traditional song that wryly criticizes immigration, such as "Mamma mia dammi cento lire."

GINGER enters. When ANNA sees GINGER, she stops her work, irritated. He takes off his coat, shivers a bit.

GINGER: Are you the laundress?

ANNA: What do you think?

GINGER smiles. ANNA is not amused.

ANNA: What smells so bad?

GINGER: 'Tis my coat. I was hoping to pay you to launder it.

ANNA inspects the coat, horrified.

GINGER: I know it's bad. I threw myself onto a man. 'Bout a week ago. He caught fire. At the smelter. T'weren't any blankets. Water didn't help – 'twas a chemical fire –

ANNA: That smelter, it is not a candy factory. You threw yourself onto a man ... on fire. You are brave or stupid. Which one?

GINGER: Couldn't say.

ANNA: It will not be easy to fix.

GINGER: I'll pay you for your trouble.

> *GINGER offers ANNA some money. She is impressed with the amount. She takes the coat and begins scrubbing.*

ANNA: The man. Is he alive?

GINGER: Aye. He'll be right.

> *GINGER looks about, then goes to touch a sheet that's hanging on the line.*

ANNA: Do not touch that, mister.

GINGER: Why not?

ANNA: It will fall apart in your hand. I hung it up this morning. The smelter has been dumping out fumes all day. Now look at it.

GINGER: If the fumes do that to the sheet, what do they do to us?

> *GINGER holds up an ashen leaf.*

GINGER: Yesterday, this rhubarb leaf was green and shining in the sun. I noticed its loveliness on the way to work. Now it crumbles in my hand. (*pause*) I saw a man "leaded" yesterday.

ANNA: Yes. Is terrible.

GINGER: He was on the ground screaming, kicking, from the pain.

ANNA: Yes. They cannot ... how you say ... digest. They cannot shit. Oh, I'm sorry, mister.

GINGER: You speak true.

ANNA: What can do we, mister? That is how it is here. Why do you not know this?

GINGER: I have only been in Trail a few months.

ANNA: Why are you not fighting in the war?

GINGER: Got black lung.

ANNA: Were you a coal miner?

GINGER: Aye. A collier. Mule drivin'.

ANNA: My big brother, Luigi, he is in the war. In the trenches. Mister, we may not like the air. But the smelter is very important. They need zinc to make the bullets. My brother Luigi needs those bullets to save his life.

Silence.

GINGER: 'As tha heard from him?

ANNA: He sends us letters. We send him bread. And wine. I hope he like.

GINGER: I am sure it is a treasure to him.

ANNA: Are you new? At the hotel?

GINGER: I rented a room. Today's events indicate I don't want to be in company accommodation. Name's Ginger. Ginger Goodwin.

ANNA: (*holding up Ginger's coat*) I need to soak it. Come back tomorrow.

GINGER: Ta. I will. Ta. That's "thank you" in Yorkshire. That's where I'm from. Tha's Italian?

ANNA: From Calabria.

GINGER: Is it nice there?

ANNA: My papa and mama say so. Trail is all I know.

GINGER: May I ask your name?

ANNA: Anna. Anna Petroni.

GINGER tips his cap and smiles.

GINGER: How do you do?

ANNA smiles awkwardly. GINGER starts to exit. As he leaves, she shouts after him.

ANNA: Drink the ginger water. In the bucket in the corner at the smelter. It will keep you from getting leaded.

GINGER: I will. Ta, Miss Petroni.

He exits. ANNA looks after him, gets a bit of a pang in her heart for him, but shakes it off.

ANNA: No one ever asks my name. No one stops to talk to laundry.

ACT ONE – Scene Three
PRINCIPESSA

Meeting Ginger has awakened a reverie in ANNA, infused with a memory of a happier time, and bathing the stage with shimmering light. In a memory: LUIGI Petroni enters and gestures to ANNA.

LUIGI: Anna, principessa, come dance. You must learn.

> *LUIGI puts his hands behind his back and starts dancing the Calabrian tarantella. ANNA joins in, swirling her skirts. LUIGI reaches his arms for hers, spinning her into the whirl of the dance.*

ANNA: Luigi?!

LUIGI: All principessas must dance. Dancing spins away your troubles. (*whirling her in the fast folk dance*) A one, two, three – hold on, Anna! My principessa. I have a dream that you will never have a burden of too much work, and you' hands will never become sore. I dream you will always have enough to eat. I dream you find love. Great love. When you dance, Anna, you remember my dream. My darling girl. My Anna.

ANNA: (*starting to cry*) Sì, Luigi, sì. You are the best brother a girl could want.

> *LUIGI dances off. ANNA spins alone, then exits.*

ACT ONE – Scene Four
DESTINY

GINGER enters. He writes in a little notebook. Lights shift. In a memory: MARY ANN enters.

MARY ANN: Would you dance with me, lad?

GINGER: Why so happy, Mum?

MARY ANN: Nothing left to be but happy, so much sorrow I done come out the other side.

GINGER: Is he –

MARY ANN: The baby's gone, gone. Another little brother. Gone. He's gone like the brother before him and the brother before him – I canna dance with them in my arms no more. Tha's one of the living ones, Ginger. Let's dance while we can. Till the mine gets you. Tha wants to be a man, like your dad, 'course you do. A man like the rest of 'em. Dontcha.

GINGER: Course I do, Mum. Seems an adventure down there.

MARY ANN: Adventure? Gaw. My mum went down pit. Dragged me and all her little babies behind her. We were little children, throwin' bits of coal into our wagon. To keep the rich man warm, while the likes of us are down in the dank, the dark, the cold. Like most of the ladies down there, my mum drunk herself to death. Now they've banned women and their little babies from the adventure, as you call it.

GINGER: Sorry, Mum. I didna know.

MARY ANN: That's why I want tha to become educated on your social conditions. Tha got the brains for it, me lad. Ginger. I want to keep tha from being covered with the dirt of the grave. I want to keep tha from breathin' that black dust that kills tha. I want to keep tha from being a man used by other men to light and heat their homes. Tha makes the world go, laddie. It's not your destiny to dig the rich man's coal. Tha's meant for grand things. Grand things, Ginger.

GINGER: Why do you dance so slow, Mum?

MARY ANN: Got nothing left, that's why, laddie. Tired in my bones. That's why.

MARY ANN dances off. GINGER exits.

ACT ONE – Scene Five
ROSE

The home of SELWYN Blaylock. SELWYN enters and sits at a small breakfast table, taking care not to wrinkle his impeccably pressed trousers. He rings a small bell, then crisply opens his newspaper. ANNA enters, wearing white gloves and carrying a tray with a fresh rose in a vase and a coffee set-up.

She waits on SELYWN with extreme care and precision.
SELYWN is pleased.

SELWYN: Mrs. Blaylock has trained you rather well.

ANNA sets the vase on the table.

SELWYN: Oh my, a rose in winter? How ever was this managed?

ANNA: Forgive me, Mr. Blaylock, am I to answer you?

SELWYN: (*laughing, charmed*) Oh yes, of course. I am the sort of
employer who encourages his employees to speak. Even housemaids.

ANNA: Yes, sir. The rose? Mrs. Blaylock has them shipped in, by train,
on ice, to please you.

SELWYN: What a grand gesture! (*pause*) You aren't the usual girl.

ANNA: I work on the weekends. Mrs. Blaylock says she needs the help.

SELWYN: She does. I fear she overexerts herself when she is … when
she is … expecting. We have lost two already. Failure to … failure …
to thrive. I couldn't bear it if we were to lose another. I couldn't. I do
not usually like to reveal things of a personal nature. But will you help?
Do you promise?

ANNA: I promise. I work hard, Mr. Blaylock.

She curtsies; he nods, then opens the newspaper.

SELWYN: Thank you. Glad to hear it.

ANNA stands, transfixed by the paper, unable to move.

SELWYN: What is it? You may speak.

ANNA: Mr. Blaylock, do you mind if I ask you a question?

SELWYN: Not at all.

ANNA: Is my brother in the list of the wounded? Would you look?

SELWYN: Of course. What's his name?

ANNA: Luigi Petroni, sir.

SELWYN: Your family should be proud.

ANNA: We are, sir.

SELWYN: Was he one of the first to sign up?

ANNA: No, he was too young. He signed up as soon as he could. He got one of your gold watches.

SELWYN: Excellent.

ANNA: That was very kind, sir. Giving them gold watches.

SELWYN: It was the least I could do. Well, my dear, you and your family can breathe a sigh of relief. He's not here.

ANNA: Oh! (*almost overwhelmed with tears*) Thank you, sir.

SELWYN: Do you mind if I ask you a question?

ANNA: No, Mr. Blaylock. It would be my honour.

SELWYN: How did you vote?

ANNA: Pardon me?

SELWYN: In the last election?

ANNA: I can't vote.

SELWYN: Oh, yes you can. All women across Canada can vote.

ANNA: Not me.

SELWYN: Why not?

ANNA: I'm twenty, sir. And Italian. You have to be twenty-one. And a British Citizen.

SELWYN: I see. I hope you will consider becoming a citizen. I know this may amaze you, but my father and mother weren't wealthy. Anything is possible in this great country. Especially for hard workers and fast learners like you. Not like some.

SELWYN angrily throws the newspaper on the floor.

ANNA: Did I do something wrong?

SELWYN: No. It's this new fellow at the smelter. He's not a brave patriot like your brother. He's led some sort of vote for a strike. We don't need troublemakers like this when we're trying to pull together for the war effort. His name is Albert Goodwin. But I hear they call him Ginger. He troubles me a great deal. A very great deal. Depriving your brother of bullets during wartime? Pure madness. I see you are as appalled as I am.

ANNA: (*shocked*) I am, Mr. Blaylock. Do you need anything else?

SELWYN: No, my dear. Thank you.

SELWYN hands ANNA the paper.

SELWYN: A present.

ANNA: For me?

SELWYN: Yes. For when you can vote.

ANNA: Oh my. Thank you.

ANNA is overcome by his kindness and his manners.

ACT ONE – Scene Six
POISON

GINGER, at the banks of the Columbia River. He is curled in a ball, in despair. JOE enters with two fishing rods, singing the traditional Yorkshire song "Old Grimy."

JOE: (*singing*) Why do these bugs torment me so?
Ah nivver did 'em 'arm:
The' come ti me when Ah'm asleep,
Aye thousands in a swarm –
(*speaking*) Ginger?

GINGER: Joe!

GINGER rises, delighted to see JOE, and laughs.

JOE: I went lookin' for tha – I had to wonder if tha'd gone daft.

GINGER: How's that, Joe?

JOE: What's tha doing out here, at this lovely river, without thy fishing rod?

GINGER: Contemplatin'.

JOE: No point in doin' that without thy fishing tackle.

GINGER: What's tha doin' here, Joe?

JOE: I can't have tha leadin' the roughest strike in the world right now by thy lonesome now, can I?

They hug.

JOE: Oh my, tha looks terrible. Tha must be leading a strike.

GINGER: Joe! Truly, what are you doing here? Duties to do with being president?

JOE: President? Tha makes me sound like Teddy Roosevelt or Woodrow Wilson, when alls I am is –

GINGER: President of all the unions of our province!

JOE: Stop. I don't want my head to swell. I likes this cap and it's almost too small now.

GINGER: Oh Joe, I am so glad to see tha.

JOE: I was in Nelson for a meeting – my position keeps me busy – a sign of the times.

GINGER: A great sign. Working men are risin' up, here, there, and everywhere.

JOE: What are you contemplatin'?

GINGER: Joe, I'm not sure I'm up to this.

JOE: Tha is, lad. Tha is. (*holding out GINGER's fishing rod*) Why don't tha tries the fishin' cure.

GINGER: Not here, Joe.

JOE: Why not?

GINGER: We're downriver from the smelter. They dump a lot of slag. Mercury, sulphur, and the like. Poisons the fish.

JOE: Right. Too bad. 'Tis a lovely river.

> *JOE practises some casts, while GINGER watches.*

GINGER: 'Tis.

JOE: I say we throw those poison fishies back. We got to fish. It'll clear our souls right out.

> *GINGER practises a cast.*

JOE: Nothin' better, right?

GINGER: Nothin'.

JOE: Tha's up to this strike, Ginger. I asked tha to come to Trail for a reason. Tha has been through the worst strikes of the century.

GINGER: Plenty had it as rough as me.

JOE: Not many. (*pause*) Tha just lost thy hope a bit.

GINGER: I can't bear the thought of my men being beaten by troops. Of children starvin'.

JOE: I don't know what to tell tha. That's leadership, Ginger. This time it will be different.

GINGER: Why?

JOE: Tha's forgettin'. Even during this terrible war, the workers overthrew the tsars of Russia! Women got the vote. Tha's forgettin' the French Revolution. We're going to get their attention this time. We're at the centre of their war, and we've stopped producing their bullets. Tha's likely in for a tough time, but tha's ready. I bet this goes all the way to the king of England.

GINGER: Go on.

JOE: Tha knows I know my labour history. I know my Marx. I know my Engels. I read everything about France and more about Russia.

GINGER: Tha does. But really, all the way to the king?

JOE: Imagine, Ginger, he might be cursing your name right now.

> *GINGER laughs.*

JOE: There's the Ginger I know. Talk to the men. Take their concerns –

GINGER: I know: one by one.

> *JOE, proud of him, claps GINGER on the shoulder.*

JOE: This river's bunky. We didna catch a thing. Except your courage.

GINGER: Aye.

JOE: You know I'm with tha. I'm watching carefully.

GINGER: Ta.

JOE: Tha's like family.

GINGER: We are family out here.

JOE: We're stuck together.

GINGER: I for one am glad for it.

JOE: Me too.

GINGER: You know who had it worse than me, Joe?

JOE: Who?

GINGER: Awd Grimy.

JOE laughs.

GINGER: I can always do with a song from back home.

JOE: Tha shall have one, then.

They exit, singing "Old Grimy":

JOE and GINGER: (*singing*) Awd Grimy's great big bug was stuffed
An' put upon a shelf,
An' if ye want another verse
Ye can mack it up yerself.

ACT ONE – Scene Seven

STELLA

ANNA enters, hauling buckets of water. She pours them into her laundry equipment. GINGER enters and offers to help, but ANNA shrugs him off. She marches over to get his jacket off the line, then hands it to GINGER. He puts it on, extremely impressed – it's like new. He touches it, pleased.

GINGER: Ta. (*pause*) Thank you. (*pause*) Why won't you speak to me?

ANNA: You organize the strikes.

GINGER: Aye.

ANNA: Strikes are trouble.

GINGER: Does the strike bring trouble? Or was the trouble there before?

ANNA: Why did you come here?

GINGER: For work.

ANNA: Why?

GINGER: I was blacklisted.

ANNA: Trouble. You're an agitator. Like Mr. Blaylock says.

GINGER: Selwyn Blaylock?

ANNA: Yes. I work for him on the weekends.

GINGER: At the mansion? At the top of the hill?

ANNA: Right.

GINGER: It must be nice there.

ANNA: You are depriving my brother of bullets! Ones Luigi needs to save his life!

GINGER: I care greatly for the soldiers, Miss Petroni.

ANNA: How's that?

GINGER: It's wrong for anyone to profit off of their injuries, their deaths. We should be looking out for them.

ANNA: Mr. Blaylock looks after them. He gave every soldier who signed up a gold watch. Luigi has one.

GINGER: Ever think why?

ANNA: Why? Because he's kind.

GINGER: If you say so. I suggest you think on that, Miss Petroni.

ANNA: Why would he, then?

GINGER: Tha's smart. Tha can figure it out.

ANNA: You think I am smart?

GINGER: Aye. Smart. And magic. You took my grimy old coat, cured it. How did you do it?

ANNA: I washed it the way my mama would. Not with chemicals. With soap and scrubbing. Better.

GINGER: That's grand. Most workers nowadays, well, we are a bit discouraged from usin' the old ways. From taking pride in our work. Instead we do some small thing over and over, with barely any idea why. We get doused with chemicals. Blasted with noise. Doesn't do much for the soul.

ANNA: (scoffing) The soul?

GINGER: Aye. The soul.

ANNA: The old ways don't do much for my hands. Please. Do not look.

GINGER: Nothin' to be ashamed of.

ANNA: Yes. I see what you say. The soul. Women used to meet at the river or the town square to do the laundry and sing. Now I sing only to myself.

GINGER: I used to help me mum. And we'd sing old Yorkshire songs.

ANNA: Like what?

GINGER: "Old Grimy."

ANNA laughs.

GINGER: You do all the laundry for the hotel?

ANNA: Yes. Dining-room linens, sheets. I also take in workers' clothes. I could get leaded. Their clothes are covered in lead dust. So I drink the ginger water.

GINGER: Wise. Quite a set-up you got goin'. How does it work?

ANNA: I scrub. Rinse. Wring them out. Hang them to dry. Iron. Here, fold here. Wrap in old newspaper. Tie them up with bow.

GINGER: Hard work.

ANNA: I'm lucky. To have a job.

GINGER: Me too. Lucky to be workin'. Good night.

ANNA: Buona sera. That's "good evening" in Italian.

GINGER: Buona sera.

ANNA: Aren't you gonna go in?

GINGER: I sleep under the stars when I can. Miss Petroni, what is "star" in Italian?

ANNA: "Stella."

GINGER: Buona sera, stella.

ANNA: Ha! Buona sera. Good night.

ANNA exits. GINGER stays, alone, stretches out on a bench, and falls asleep.

ACT ONE – Scene Eight
SOMEBODY

In a dream: WALTER Goodwin enters carrying his long-handled miner's pick and begins undercutting a coal seam.

GINGER: Dad, you are so strong. Toughest job in the mine.

WALTER keeps picking at the seam.

GINGER: All your mates look up to tha. Dad, why you keepin' me from the mines? I could drive mule for thee, Dad, and we could go in business together.

WALTER keeps picking at the seam, but then stops and stands with difficulty.

WALTER: Tha's a smart one, Albert. Mum says you learned to read. Mum says your teacher is from Oxford, Oxford University. Come up to teach the workers what's what. That's a gift, lad: to know not only what we are in, but why.

GINGER: But tha needs me to work, Dad. Tha needs the money.

WALTER: Albert, thee'll be a somebody, lad. Not like your dad.

GINGER: Tha's somebody, Dad –

WALTER: No, my boy, I'm a nobody.

GINGER: Not to me, Dad, not to me.

ACT ONE – Scene Nine
ABIDING

WORKERS enter. GINGER enters with a letter.

GINGER: My brothers, we have an offer.

WORKERS cheer.

GINGER: Mr. Blaylock says if we all go back to work –

WORKER 1: Aye?

GINGER: He'll get the company in to arbitrate. And he'll abide by whatever they decide.

WORKER 2: Sounds reasonable.

WORKER 3: Does.

WORKER 8: Wait – getting the company to arbitrate?

WORKER 4: The company is the one whose been giving us this terrible deal all along.

WORKER 8: Right.

WORKER 5: What sort of offer is that?

GINGER: A fast one. The first one.

WORKER 9: Abide by the company?

WORKER 6: We been abiding and abiding till we can't abide no more.

WORKER 7: And we have to stop our strike first.

WORKER 1: Abandon our position.

WORKER 2: Abandon our power.

WORKER 8: Any sign of the strike pay from the Americans?

GINGER: Not yet. I've written to them again.

WORKER 3: We should take Mr. Blaylock's offer.

WORKER 4: It's no offer.

WORKER 5: It's an insult.

WORKER 6: I can't wait for the strike pay.

WORKER 7: Christmas is coming. What about my children?

WORKER 3: You will take better care of your children if we win this thing.

WORKER 7: I got no savings.

GINGER: Is there anyone here who can help this fellow?

WORKER 8: What do you need?

WORKER 7: I got nothing to eat.

WORKER 2: We'll feed you. Come on by.

WORKER 7: I'm not a beggar or a shirker.

WORKER 5: We know.

WORKER 6: There's no shame in it.

GINGER: They are the ones who should be ashamed. It is their carelessness that led to our strike. My brothers. You look disheartened. I'm not. Why? Because that was the fastest offer I've ever seen anywhere, in any strike. They're paying attention. Shall we vote? Yes or no to Mr. Blaylock's offer.

> *WORKERS agree. They vote. It's a no.*

GINGER: It's a no.

> *WORKERS cheer.*

WORKER 8: I want to go back to work.

WORKER 2: We've voted. Stick with us. Save your grumblin' for the company.

GINGER: My brothers and sisters, stay strong.

ACT ONE – Scene Ten
SIGNATURE

> *Later at night, on the back porch of the Meakin Hotel, a sleepless GINGER is trying to find solace and strength by gazing at the night sky. ANNA enters, trembling from a terrible dream, and holding the newspaper Selwyn gave her earlier, as if it could bring her luck.*

GINGER: What are you doing up?

ANNA: (*shuddering*) Nightmares.

GINGER: About your brother?

> *ANNA nods, terrified.*

ANNA: Luigi ... They say letters mean so much to the soldiers, but I cannot write.

GINGER: I'll teach tha.

ANNA: You would?

GINGER: 'Course.

ANNA: I know my alphabet.

GINGER: How about we start with you signing your name?

ANNA: Me? Sign my name? In handwriting?

GINGER: Aye. It's not so hard. Here's a pen.

ANNA: "Write." It's a lovely word.

GINGER: Agreed. Now. What shall you write on? Might we use this? (*pointing to Blaylock's newspaper, but then seeing ANNA's hesitancy*) In the margins.

ANNA: No. I want to keep it nice.

GINGER: It's been ironed. Where did tha get this? Mr. Blaylock?

ANNA nods.

GINGER: He's giving you gifts.

ANNA nods once more.

GINGER: (*gesturing to the newspaper she wraps laundry in*) What about these?

ANNA: No. Oh, no. They'll notice they're missing.

GINGER: Here.

ANNA: Oh, I cannot. It's such nice paper.

GINGER: 'Tis only old union letterhead.

ANNA: Oh no. You'll need.

GINGER: Anna, you've got to use something if you are going to learn to write. 'Tis a gift. You accept them from Mr. Blaylock. I'll be offended if tha won't take it.

ANNA takes the paper.

GINGER: Here's how you write an *A*.

GINGER carefully traces a cursive capital A.

ANNA: (*laughing*) It's like a loop, with a dog's tail.

GINGER sees what she sees and laughs as well.

GINGER: 'Tis. Here, you try.

ANNA tries.

GINGER: Why haven't I seen a single dog in Trail?

ANNA: They die here.

GINGER: Oh. That's awful.

ANNA: From the smelter fumes. From eating the grass. It's cruel to bring them here.

GINGER: Terrible. (*pause*) Anna, there's a grand *A*!

ANNA smiles.

GINGER: Now all you need is an *n*.

He shows her how to write it.

ANNA: It's like a feather on the wind, blowing up against a mountain.

GINGER: Why, Miss Petroni, tha's a poet! Try.

ANNA does.

GINGER: Now there's a lovely *n*. To write your name, all you do is put it all together.

ANNA tries.

GINGER: Right, right.

ANNA: One world with dog's tail, two mountains with feathers on the wind ... another world ... dog tail ... I did it! I did it!

GINGER: You did.

ANNA: Grazie.

GINGER: How do you say "you're welcome" in Italian?

ANNA: "Prego."

GINGER: Prego, Miss Petroni.

ANNA is overcome with joy. She and GINGER smile at each other.

ANNA: Good night.

GINGER: Buona sera.

ANNA: I must go in. Is late, Mr. Goodwin.

ACT ONE – Scene Eleven
LIGHT

SELWYN is practising his speech for ANNA. She is holding a telegram for him on a tray.

SELWYN: "Before electricity, we dwelt in the dark, huddled around dim and dripping candles, in fear for our very lives. Many a building, many a town, burned to the ground by tragic fire. Now Trail is ablaze with modern street lights and entirely safe. Isn't it marvellous?"

ANNA: It is, sir.

SELWYN: "Now all of us, *all of us*, can work at any time, day or night. The profits, the possibilities, are without limit. We are like Edison with his light bulb. We are like the alchemists of old – with one crucial difference. We can turn zinc to gold."

ANNA: (*quietly*) Un risultato notevole.

SELWYN: English only, please. In the house, at any rate.

ANNA: I am sorry, Mr. Blaylock.

> *SELWYN notices ANNA is carrying a telegram and reaches out for it.*

SELWYN: What was it you said, in Italian? "Risulto ..." Result? "Nota-nota–" Notable?

ANNA: Sir, is more like ... "Remarkable. Achievement."

SELWYN: Thank you. What do you think of my speech?

> *ANNA is completely stunned he would ask her this.*

ANNA: (*nodding several times*) Sì.

SELWYN: (*shaking his head – not Italian again!*) No!

ANNA: Very good.

SELWYN: I hope you will be able to help serve at the party.

ANNA: Yes. It would be my honour.

SELWYN: Scientists and industrialists from all over the world are coming.

ANNA: To Trail?!

SELWYN: Yes.

SELWYN notices ANNA is still holding a telegram for him on a tray; he reaches for it and opens it.

SELWYN: Hmm. Wonderful, wonderful.

SELWYN drops the telegram on the tray.

SELWYN: On second thought, I'll save that. Not every day you hear from the prime minister, now is it?

ANNA shakes her head, nods, then curtsies.

ACT ONE – Scene Twelve
RISKS

A party atmosphere in the Union Hall. GINGER, JOE, and WORKERS are drinking beer, eating soup, and singing Ralph Chaplin's 1915 anthem "Solidarity Forever."

WORKERS: When the union's inspiration through the workers'
blood shall run,
There can be no power greater anywhere beneath the sun;
Yet what force on earth is weaker than the feeble strength of one,
For the Union makes us strong.
(*chorus*)
Solidarity forever,
Solidarity forever,
Solidarity forever,
For the Union makes us strong.

GINGER pulls JOE aside.

GINGER: The American Union hasn't sent their strike pay.

JOE: Not yet?

GINGER: No.

JOE: Have you got their commitment in writing?

GINGER: (*showing JOE a letter*) Aye.

JOE: (*handing the letter back*) Looks right enough.

GINGER: Joe, have I –

JOE: Don't be doubting yourself. Now's not the time. Those fellows were dying at work, getting leaded, ropes breaking, platforms falling on them, killing them, while this company makes record profits. You're working to change that. Don't forget.

GINGER: Aye.

JOE: How is their morale?

The WORKERS are still drinking and singing.

GINGER: Seems good enough. Ta for paying for this party.

JOE: You're welcome.

GINGER: Seems to be lifting their spirits.

The WORKERS resume singing the chorus of "Solidarity Forever," a bit drunkenly.

A WORKER stumbles over to them.

WORKER: Thanks Ginger, thanks Joe.

JOE: Thank you for standing strong.

WORKER: I am, aren't I, standing strong!

The WORKER laughs and goes back into the crowd to sing.

GINGER: Word is Selwyn Blaylock wrote to the premier, and he wrote to the prime minister.

JOE: Straight to the top, eh? They never gave a damn about us coal miners.

GINGER: Do you think they'll send in strikebreakers? I don't think I could bear to see my men beaten.

JOE: That's the risks, Ginger.

GINGER: I know, but –

JOE: You go talk to 'em. Keep their spirits up.

GINGER: Aye. (*standing to speak*) I want to thank Joe for this party, for the ale and the food.

The WORKERS shout.

GINGER: But more importantly, I want to thank him for bringing us together. My brothers, my sisters, we are engaged in one of the toughest fights the world has ever seen. Selwyn Blaylock and his like do not care for your safety, your security, your health, or your well-being. Mr. Blaylock and his bosses do not care if you live or die. They make money off the death of our brothers in their trenches. But are you letting them run roughshod over you? No. You are standing up for yourselves and for workers everywhere. If we persevere, the eight-hour day shall become law. If we preserve, workers shall be treated decently. If we preserve, we will win the day!

ALL cheer.

JOE: More slape ale to slocken your thirst in the back!

WORKER: What?

JOE: More ale in the back!

ALL exit, cheering at the idea of free beer.

ACT ONE – Scene Thirteen

TARANTELLA

GINGER brings a typewriter out to the laundry area, where ANNA is waiting.

ANNA: What you got there?

GINGER: A typewriter. We can write to Luigi. If tha has the time.

ANNA: Write to Luigi? Oh. He'll be so surprised. What do I do?

GINGER: Sit here.

ANNA: (*sitting in front of the typewriter*) I have his package. I will put my letter with the socks and the bread and the Vino Calabrese. What do I do?

GINGER: See the alphabet?

ANNA: I do. I press, it make the letter, no?

GINGER: Yes. Miss Petroni. "Dear" is *d-e-a-r.*

ANNA: (*typing*) Oh look. Look!

GINGER: And you know how to spell "Luigi."

She types l-u-i-g-i.

ANNA: (*reading*) "Dear Luigi …" Ha! Now what?

GINGER: Write what you like.

ANNA: I do not know. What do you think he's doing?

GINGER: (*sighing heavily at the thought*) I believe it is better to tell him stories from home, Miss Petroni.

ANNA: About what? The strike? Too much worry.

GINGER: You could write about your beau.

ANNA: Oh. I do not have.

GINGER: There's a surprise.

ANNA: I work all the time. My hands are red, raw. No man want.

GINGER: No worker would hold that against tha.

ANNA: Are your wife's hands like this?

GINGER: No.

ANNA: Oh, what are they like?

GINGER: I don't have a wife. I cannot.

ANNA: Why?

GINGER: Union organizers, we get death threats. Same for our families. I don't want a wife to face that. So I'd best be out of the whole thing – love.

ANNA: That's a lot to give up.

GINGER: 'Tis.

ANNA: I don't know what to write to Luigi.

GINGER: He'd like to hear about your parents.

ANNA: He would?

GINGER: I'm sure of it. I wish I could see mine. Been over thirteen years now. My mum used to dote on me. And me dad, what I would give for a visit.

ANNA: My papa danced last night. The tarantella.

GINGER: Luigi would love to hear about that.

ANNA tries to type "Papa" but gets frustrated.

ANNA: I type too slow. Would you do?

GINGER: 'Course.

GINGER: (*reading*) "Papa" … (*typing some more*) "danced the" – (*pause*) "Tarantella." That's the devil to spell, Miss Petroni. I hope it's easier to dance.

ANNA shows him. They finally collapse laughing and ANNA kisses GINGER on the cheek. He is embarrassed but very glad. He hands her the letter for her to sign. She puts it in Luigi's package and exits. He looks after her and sighs.

GINGER writes in his journal, stopping to think.

Lights change.

ACT ONE – Scene Fourteen
THEN THERE ARE THE STARS

In a dream: On a bench outside, GINGER joins WALTER, who is returning home after his work shift.

GINGER: (*as a fifteen-year-old boy*) Dad, how ever did you survive those strikes?

WALTER: Broke my heart. I had to take you down pit with me. We didna have the money for you to learn no more.

GINGER: It's all right, Dad. I can take care of a mule for you so ya don't have to wait for the mule driver any more. Going down, down into the dark, Dad – I canna get the mule to budge!

WALTER: Coax the mule. Carrots are better than sticks. The poor animals never see the light of day. 'Tis a pitiable life. 'Cept during the strike, we let 'em run free in the fields – lovely to see. And they deserve some kindness, lad.

GINGER: Aye, Dad. There I was, you cutting new coal out of the seam, and me and my mule hauling it out, you and me runnin' our own business, Dad. Dad, it's hard, comin' into the mine when it's dark outside, and leavin' when it's dark outside, dark all day inside the mine, we never see a scrap of light.

WALTER: But then there are the stars.

GINGER and WALTER gaze at the beauty of the stars. Then WALTER begins coughing.

GINGER: You right there, Dad?

WALTER: Black lung. Keep that kerchief over your face, boy. Keeps the coal dust out. As best as we can.

GINGER: All these men around us murmuring prayers not to die. The mothers were cryin' because they didn't have the money to feed their children. Dad, we aren't runnin' our own business, are we?

WALTER: No son, we aren't. The company's runnin' us.

GINGER: I want to do somethin' about it, Dad.

WALTER: You do that, Ginger. You're my fine lad.

GINGER: Aye. I will, Dad.

ACT ONE – Scene Fifteen
FEAST

ANNA is cleaning SELWYN's small table. ELSIE, a chorus girl, stumbles out and readjusts her skirt. She laughs and shrieks when she sees ANNA, who is overwhelmed and shocked by her.

ELSIE: Oh my. They're all so grabby.

ELSIE sees a stain on her dress, grabs a napkin off of the table that ANNA is cleaning, spits on it, and tries to scrub the stain off.

ELSIE: Stains of gentlemen. Ewhk. Don't be so high and mighty, miss. You think my outfit goads them on? I saw them grabbing you, too, and you're dressed like a nun. Might as well get paid for it. You're a looker. Ever thought of goin' into showbiz? Sing with me.

ELSIE bursts into song: it's a modified version of Irving Berlin's 1918 "Oh! How I Hate to Get Up in the Morning." ANNA sings along, reluctantly, at ELSIE's constant urging.

ELSIE: (*singing*)[7] I've been a smelterman a while
And I would like to state
The life is simply wonderful
The lead 'n zinc is great

> *ELSIE goes on singing the song's chorus but eventually acknowledges ANNA's lack of enthusiasm.*

ELSIE: What's wrong, sister?

ANNA: They're making fun of the smelter workers.

ELSIE: So? What did ya expect?

ANNA: They're feasting. On cake.

ELSIE: Don't they always?

ANNA: I thought they were gentlemen.

ELSIE: All blokes like a slap and a tickle. (*peeking back in at the party*) Oh, damn. Can't go back downstairs now. Mr. Blaylock is making his speech. Lead from bullets becoming gold. All electric light. Blah blah blah.

> *We hear SELWYN and catch a glimpse of him. ELSIE makes fun of him. ANNA is increasingly disgusted.*

ANNA: We should have a piece of that gold. We should have a piece of that light.

ELSIE: A rebel girl, eh?

ANNA: A what?

ELSIE: Ask around.

ANNA: What is it? Please tell me.

ELSIE: It's a song. Sweetie, if I'm going to rise in the ranks and become a star, I've got to go back in there.

> *ANNA nods and exits. ELSIE starts to leave, but then collapses in a chair and has a drink.*

---

7   Alternate lyrics from an unknown author – one of dozens of parodies of the version sung by Berlin in the 1943 musical comedy *This Is the Army*, directed by Michael Curtiz.

ACT ONE – Scene Sixteen
REBEL GIRL

GINGER sings the first verse of Joe Hill's 1915 song "The Rebel Girl" to ANNA.

GINGER: (*singing*) There are women of many descriptions
In this queer world, as everyone knows.
Some are living in beautiful mansions,
And are wearing the finest of clothes.
There are blue-blood queens and princesses,
Who have charms made of diamonds and pearl,
But the only and thoroughbred lady
Is the Rebel Girl.

ANNA: That is why she called me a rebel girl.

GINGER: Tha is!

ANNA: I been thinking about what you said. About the gold watch. Soldiers need bullets very much. The company and Mr. Blaylock make a big profit. With such profit, a gold watch cost them nothing.

GINGER: Right.

ANNA: But there is one thing I not understand. You help explain?

GINGER: 'Course.

ANNA: Why does Mr. Blaylock drive the workers so hard? It is too much for my papa.

GINGER: Supply, demand, and social conditions. It's like a great swirl, and we're all in it, and you can suddenly see it. If we can see it, we can change it.

ANNA: Supply, demand. My papa work hard because there is a war, and there is a demand for bullets.

GINGER: Right. And they've got to make as much profit, as quickly as they can, because …

ANNA: The war may end. Then there will be no demand for bullets.

GINGER: Right.

ANNA: Now they are desperate for bullets. So they can charge a lot of money. (*pause*) They have no reason for the war to end.

GINGER: No, they don't. War is part of capitalism.

ANNA: What hope is there?

GINGER: If we can see it, we can change it. A man named Karl Marx saw that we don't just sell things like bullets. We workers sell our work. We're part of supply and demand.

ANNA: We sell it to them?

GINGER: We do.

ANNA: And if you strike, you create a demand.

GINGER: We do.

ANNA: Mr. Blaylock buys twelve, thirteen hours from my papa, but only pays him for eight. If we strike, if we fight, we can demand to work eight hours and be paid for eight hours. I see how your dream works.

GINGER: I have many more.

ANNA: Tell me.

GINGER: Imagine if no worker would kill another worker. The war would be over tomorrow. Imagine if the government sends in the federal fair-wage officer to mediate our strike. That will mean a new day for us workers.

ANNA: That's worth fighting for.

GINGER: Ta.

    ANNA is very moved.

ANNA: Mr. Goodwin. You have so many dreams for workers. Do you have any dreams for yourself?

GINGER: Not really, Miss Petroni.

ANNA: Anna.

GINGER: Anna.

ANNA: Maybe there will come a day … when the workers you fight for will have what they need. And you'll be free.

GINGER: There is nothing I hope for more.

ACT TWO – Scene One
FEATHER

FRANCES hands white feathers to male passersby on the boardwalk, one by one. As they pass, they accept the feathers but brush past, ignoring her.

FRANCES: Shirker. Slacker. (*to GINGER*) Coward.

GINGER: I may be many things, madam, but I am no coward.

FRANCES: What do you call opening the gates to madmen and leaving our homes defenceless? You should be fighting with our boys.

GINGER: I'm category D, ma'am. I got ulcers from the strikes. Black lung. The food alone would kill me.

FRANCES: Strikes? You have to get back to work! This strike is depriving our boys of bullets! Get back to work. Back. To. Work.

GINGER: Have you a son over there, ma'am?

FRANCES: Three, I'll have you know.

GINGER: I wish you all the best, I do.

FRANCES: Do you believe in slavery everlasting for the Kaiser's sake, amen?

GINGER: I believe in freedom from wage slavery.

FRANCES dumps feathers on GINGER.

FRANCES: You obliterate all feelings of wrath and indignation for crimes against humanity and civilization. You and your strike support a supine endurance of all insults, a cringing compliance with the vile forces of bestiality, destruction, and lust, in milk-and-water namby-pambyism and flapdoodle, in gush and bunkum, in veiled eyes and in soft heads, in the encouragement of cowardice, in the forgiveness of everything rotten –

GINGER: Ma'am, ma'am.

FRANCES starts sobbing.

GINGER: I believe a worker should not kill another worker.

FRANCES starts crying. GINGER pats her on the arm, and she collapses in his arms, sobbing.

FRANCES: When will this strike end?

GINGER: I don't know, ma'am.

FRANCES: My boys, my boys. Will they come back?

GINGER: I don't know, ma'am. I'm sorry. So very sorry.

ACT TWO – Scene Two
BONSAI

SELWYN is cutting a small bonsai tree. He is having difficulty pruning and tying it back. He rings a bell. ANNA enters.

ANNA: Yes, Mr. Blaylock?

SELWYN: My dear, would you hold this branch? Here? Take off your gloves. You don't want to dirty them. No, like this. (*twisting the branch, pruning it*) There, thank you. Oh my, your hands.

ANNA: From laundry.

SELWYN: Oh. (*reaching into his pocket*) I have some salve I've been working on. Put it on now. Tell me if it works.

ANNA: You invented this?

SELWYN: I did.

ANNA: Oh. It feels better.

SELWYN: Excellent.

ANNA: They say you invented the kind of smelting we do now.

SELWYN: Correct.

ANNA: It must be a wonderful feeling.

SELWYN: It is. (*confiding*) The premier, the prime minister, even the king of England, they say they want to tour my facilities.

ANNA: The king?

SELWYN: Yes. I'll have to build a mansion. A summer home. To entertain them. Imagine. With glorious gardens. The Japanese industrialist gave me this bonsai tree to start my garden. What do you think?

ANNA: It is small.

SELWYN: It's meant to be. "Bonsai," it's called. Any tree can be this small if you train it, and cut it.

ANNA: (*jumping at the sound of the wind rattling the windows*) Oh!

SELWYN: The wind. It's strong up here, on top of the hill. It frightens you.

ANNA: Yes.

SELWYN: Good. Hold this branch, would you? Those down in the valley, the workers don't think of that. We have to withstand high winds up here, in management.

ANNA: Mr. Blaylock. Do you mind if I ask you –

SELWYN: Hold this piece, please, while I secure it. (*wrapping the branch with wire*) Ask away.

ANNA: Do you believe workers deserve a piece of your light?

SELWYN: Of course. The street lights are for all.

ANNA: I mean do you believe workers deserve a piece of the profits?

SELWYN: Of course not. That is socialist. Communist. We live in a free world.

ANNA: I not understand.

SELWYN: I am responsible to shareholders, scientists, workers, science itself. The company would not operate without a profit. Everyone in Trail would lose their jobs. I am responsible to the soldiers. I serve on the Draft Board. I'm on the Board of Trade.

ANNA: But the safety in the smelter, the long hours –

SELWYN: I am sorry, my dear, but my home is my respite. I must ask you to stop this strike talk.

ANNA: Yes, Mr. Blaylock.

SELWYN: How is that salve working? Let me see. (*taking her hands*) Hmm. Do they still hurt?

ANNA: No. It works very good. Thank you.

ANNA goes to hand it back.

SELWYN: I'm so glad. Keep it.

ANNA: Thank you, sir.

SELWYN: Say, I almost forgot. I hear your brother is due home any day. How is he?

ANNA: (*tearing up*) What? I – How?

SELWYN: He's been injured.

ANNA: Oh. (*pause*) Injured. How bad?

SELWYN: (*lying*) They didn't say. (*handing ANNA an envelope of money*) This is for him.

ANNA looks inside and gasps.

SELWYN: It's the least I could do. And please tell him that there is a job waiting for him at the smelter, when he's ready. I'm looking out for him.

ANNA: (*starting to weep and barely able to speak*) Thank you.

SELWYN smiles at her, kindly.

ACT TWO – Scene Three

WORSE

GINGER, on the street. A WORKER rushes up to speak to him. He is soon joined by many WORKERS surrounding him.

WORKER 1: Ginger!

GINGER stops.

WORKER 1: May I have a word?

GINGER: Of course.

WORKER 1: I can't keep on. If I were back in Italy, I would be eating from my garden. But the fumes from the smelter have ruined it.

WORKER 2: We need food.

WORKER 3: When I voted yes for the strike, I was counting on that strike pay coming from the American Union.

WORKER 4: My children are crying for food.

WORKER 5: Mine need shoes. It's winter.

WORKER 6: My papa's eyes are like glass.

WORKER 8: My wife has nothing to cook.

WORKER 9: Do you think the federal government will send in soldiers?

WORKER 7: Will they beat us?

GINGER: Maybe not. Soldiers are scarce these days.

WORKER 7: True. Canadians have sent six hundred thousand
men over there.

WORKER 8: What have you heard?

GINGER: Nothing. I know what you know. I sent another telegram to the
American Union. I hear word of our strike has gone all the way to the
prime minister. He might send in troops.

WORKER 9: What do you hope for?

GINGER: That he sends in a federal fair-wage officer to arbitrate. That
would mean a brighter day for all us workers. That our demands matter.
That our day, of fairness and joy, is coming.

WORKER 8: All right, brother Goodwin, I'll stay steady.

GINGER: Thank you, brothers.

ACT TWO – Scene Four
LUIGI

*ANNA and GINGER enter a hospital. Nurse RITA greets
them.*

ANNA: Rita! How long you work here?

RITA: A month. They need nurses bad. Hello, Ginger.

ANNA: You know each other?

RITA: Sì. He come often to see the soldiers. It is very good for them to not
be so alone. (*pause*) You are here to see Luigi.

ANNA: Sì.

RITA: I will bring.

> *RITA exits and comes back leading LUIGI, who is blind. ANNA gasps. LUIGI coughs occasionally and winces from internal injuries.*

ANNA: Luigi –

LUIGI: Anna?

ANNA: Oh, Luigi, I am so sorry.

LUIGI: Where are Mama and Papa?

ANNA: I said I would come see you first.

LUIGI: To protect them.

ANNA: Yes.

LUIGI: Oh. Who is the man? With you.

ANNA: How you know he is here?

LUIGI: I hear his boots on the tiles.

ANNA: Will you see again?

LUIGI: They say no. What is his name?

ANNA: Oh, he is Ginger. Ginger Goodwin.

LUIGI: Ah, a man for Anna. At last. How do you do?

> *An awkward silence. But GINGER and ANNA enjoy that this might be true, for a moment.*

ANNA: He is not – he is a friend.

LUIGI: Ah, too bad. Ginger, what do you think of this ward?

GINGER: Oh, I come here often. To visit the soldiers back from the front.

LUIGI: What for?

GINGER: To educate myself. On the war. What the men go through.

LUIGI: Then you know.

ANNA: Know what?

LUIGI: He knows that war is nothing like they said it would be.

GINGER: Right.

ANNA: Well you're home now. Mr. Blaylock said you could have a job. (*pause*) What's wrong?

LUIGI: Nobody is going to give a blind man a job.

ANNA: And he gave you this money.

LUIGI takes but throws the money.

ANNA: Luigi, what are you doing? Mr. Blaylock gave you that.

LUIGI: Blood money, Anna. Made of the death of my brothers.

ANNA: Luigi –

LUIGI: And you can take his gold watch too. Take it! Take it or I'll smash it on the floor.

ANNA: Luigi –

ANNA takes the gold watch. LUIGI has a bad coughing fit.

ANNA: I don't feel right having your watch, Luigi.

LUIGI: How am I going to read it now?

There is a sad silence.

ANNA: Luigi, when you get there and you see the war is so bad –

LUIGI: What? You think I could do something? Anything? I couldn't. Because they shoot us, Anna. They shoot us if we disobey. They shoot us if we try to come home. They shoot us if we don't follow an order. (*pause*) Wait, are you that Ginger that's leading the strike?

GINGER: I am.

LUIGI: Good for you. It will help Papa.

LUIGI begins singing Carlo Tuzzi's 1908 labour song "Bandiera rossa" (Red flag). GINGER joins him. ANNA is shocked.

LUIGI and GINGER: (*singing*) Bandiera rossa la trionferà
Bandiera rossa la trionferà

ANNA: Luigi, you not sing songs like this before the war.

LUIGI: I learned, Anna. I learned.

LUIGI and GINGER: (*singing again*) Bandiera rossa la trionferà
Evviva il comunismo e la libertà!

LUIGI: That company making money off of bullets. Making money off us. Making money, making money!

GINGER: I hope that class of parasites fang themselves to death.

LUIGI laughs.

LUIGI: Anna, you got yourself a good man.

ANNA: He's not –

LUIGI: He should be, Anna. I am not going to be able to – look after you –

ANNA starts to cry. GINGER catches her eye. ANNA looks away and wipes her tears.

LUIGI: What kind of life will I have?

ANNA lets herself cry. GINGER holds her. LUIGI coughs.

ANNA: I will come back. Soon, Luigi.

ANNA and GINGER leave the hospital. RITA tends to LUIGI, then leads him off.

ACT TWO – Scene Five

DREAMS

GINGER and ANNA walk back to the porch area. They sit down. GINGER puts his arm around ANNA to comfort her. She falls asleep on his shoulder. He falls asleep, too.

In a dream: MARY ANN enters and gestures for GINGER to come dance with her.

MARY ANN: Ginger, my lad, why don't you court her?

GINGER: Mum! How can tha suggest such a thing?

MARY ANN: 'Tis nature, laddie.

GINGER: It is not nature, I fear, Mum. It is the company. It is the cruelty of man. How could I be with a woman when I see what havin' babies in a company town did to tha?

MARY ANN: It brought me thee, Albert. Me little Ginger. Tha'll make a good husband. A good father. Yer kind.

GINGER: They can threaten me, but I couldna stomach the threats comin' to Anna, to my children.

MARY ANN: I see how tha looks at children in the street.

GINGER: How's that, Mum?

MARY ANN: Like you know what yer missin'.

GINGER: I do.

> *MARY ANN and GINGER exit. In a dream: LUIGI enters, as if he were well again. ANNA rises to dance with him.*

LUIGI: I want to dance with you at your wedding.

ANNA: Oh, Luigi.

LUIGI: That man Ginger. He's not such a bad fella. Almost good as an Italian. He does much for us. Soldiers. Italians. Workers.

ANNA: He say his life is too dangerous to marry.

LUIGI: All our lives are dangerous. Anna, there aren't going to be any men your age left.

ANNA: What?

LUIGI: We are all dying.

> *ANNA stops dancing, as her heart starts to break.*

LUIGI: I want you to have love, my Anna, a family. You get him to fall in love with you. How can he not? You're my Principessa.

> *LUIGI and ANNA exit. We hear the sound of a river.*

ACT TWO – Scene Six
HERE

> *GINGER is down by the river. He paces, waiting for ANNA. She runs in.*

ANNA: Ginger. I am here. Like I promise.

GINGER: Anna. It's lovely down here, isn't it?

ANNA: It is.

GINGER: The light. It dances through the trees. On the water. Look how lovely it is, all frozen up.

ANNA: It is beautiful. (*pause*) I have to get back. To work.

GINGER: All I ask is a moment. I've been thinking about what tha said, about brighter days. When I won't have to sacrifice it all for the cause. Miss Petroni, that brighter day, it's here, or nearly so.

ANNA: What?

GINGER: Mr. Blaylock's plea to have the government step in has resulted in something clean, and fair, and wonderful.

ANNA: What?

GINGER: The prime minister is sending in a federal fair-wage officer, to mediate!

ANNA: Oh, Ginger, congratulations.

GINGER: I meet with him today.

ANNA goes to hug GINGER, but he sweeps her in an embrace and whirls her. They pause, looking at each other with great longing.

GINGER: I'm shaking –

ANNA: Me too.

GINGER kisses ANNA passionately. She kisses him back. He touches her hair, then gently unties the red ribbon holding it back. Once her hair is free, he runs his fingers through it, exploring, playful. She laughs in delight. They kiss again.

GINGER: Miss Petroni, I thought about what you said, about dreams for myself – and they're dreams for you, too – for both of us.

ANNA: Yes? Oh, yes, yes!

They kiss.

GINGER: I never thought I would ever be this happy. Anna.

ANNA: Me either. Ginger.

They hold hands and exit together. They part ways, heading for work. GINGER gently cradles ANNA's red ribbon in his hands.

ACT TWO – Scene Seven
EAT SMOKE

This scene takes place in two locales, suggested by two tables. One is Selwyn's breakfast nook; the other is a plain wooden negotiating table with three chairs. A clock ticks.

Enter SELWYN. He sits at his breakfast table, careful to keep his trousers neat. He reads the newspaper.

Enter GINGER. He sits, excitedly, at the negotiation table.

Enter STEPHEN, the federal fair-wage officer. He is a well-dressed government official. He carries a case for his documents. GINGER stands to shake STEPHEN's hand.

STEPHEN: You must be Albert Goodwin.

GINGER: I am. Right you are.

STEPHEN: Stephen Blythe. At your service.

GINGER: How do you do?

STEPHEN: I'm not allowed to discuss the particulars.

GINGER is still filled with exuberant excitement. STEPHEN begins laying out his papers, an inkwell, a pen.

GINGER: Of course not. Thank you for coming.

Pause. They shift awkwardly and look for SELWYN.

GINGER: Would you care to sit?

STEPHEN sits, then GINGER. A pause.

A clock strikes the hour at Selwyn's home: it's 10 a.m.

SELWYN rings a little bell. ANNA enters, filled with joy. She is shocked to see SELWYN at home.

SELWYN: Tea today. If you please.

Pause. ANNA is shocked and confused – isn't SELWYN supposed to be at the meeting? GINGER and STEPHEN shift in their chairs. The chairs creak.

Pause. ANNA is still rooted to the spot. This can't be happening.

SELWYN: What is it?

ANNA: Excuse me, Mr. Blaylock, don't you have an appointment?

SELWYN: What business is that of yours?

ANNA: I – I –

SELWYN: You may go.

ANNA is starting to feel very anxious. As the clock ticks, her dreams are dying. Sickened, she exits to get the tea.

STEPHEN pulls out his pocket watch and looks at it, annoyed that SELWYN isn't there.

STEPHEN: I can tell you Ottawa is sympathetic. Very.

GINGER nods, gratefully. He still believes SELWYN will show up.

The sound of a kettle whistle. Then it stops. ANNA enters with a tea service, sets it down, and waits. She can't move: her heart is breaking. ANNA gets her courage and decides to speak: it's now or never.

ANNA: Many people are pinning their hopes on you, sir.

Pause. SELWYN pours his tea. ANNA trembles. SELWYN sighs.

STEPHEN: Is there any word from Mr. Blaylock?

GINGER: No.

GINGER is feeling anxious. He tries to hide it.

STEPHEN: Was I not clear? I have the morning, and then I must catch the train back to Ottawa.

GINGER: You were clear.

STEPHEN: Is this like Mr. Blaylock?

GINGER: I know not.

ANNA is looking very nervous.

SELWYN: I thought you enjoyed working here.

ANNA: I do, sir.

SELWYN: The kindness I've shown you.

ANNA: Yes, sir.

SELWYN: And your brother.

ANNA: Yes, sir. I'm very grateful.

SELWYN: You must know what a premium I put on manners.

ANNA: I do.

SELWYN: Are you being polite?

ANNA: No. Sir.

SELWYN: I am going to ignore it, then.

> *SELWYN taps his tea cup. ANNA pours his tea.*

SELWYN: You are very good with Mrs. Blaylock. I sense that you calm her nerves, that we might even hope to have more Blaylocks running around, with your sweet countenance looking over them.

ANNA: Thank you.

SELWYN: If you must know, we don't need a union. It is already my belief that the security, comfort, and welfare of workmen will be paid for in increased efficiency and good will of employees. I give the smeltermen turkeys at Christmas. Perhaps you've eaten one.

ANNA: I have. Thank you.

> *STEPHEN looks at his pocket watch. GINGER starts to feel desperate.*

GINGER: I could arrange accommodation for you, sir.

> *Pause. GINGER tries again.*

GINGER: We could try again. Tomorrow.

STEPHEN: I simply cannot.

> *Pause.*

GINGER: I could go to Mr. Blaylock's home and remind him.

STEPHEN: What good would that do?

GINGER: Sir?

STEPHEN: I've seen it before. Managers don't ignore telegrams from the federal government without a reason. Mr. Blaylock is refusing to meet with me.

GINGER: I see.

> *STEPHEN begins packing up. GINGER is desperate and puts his hand on the papers, preventing STEPHEN from putting them in his briefcase, but STEPHEN gently removes the papers and files them neatly. GINGER turns away: he can't bear to watch.*

SELWYN: Our hockey team, the Smoke Eaters. I sponsor it for the smelter workers. Perhaps you've been to a game.

ANNA: I have, sir.

SELWYN: Great fun, aren't they?

ANNA: (*pause*) Eat smoke? Is this what we are supposed to do? Even a dog cannot live in our valley. But maybe you not know, here on the hill, safe from the poison. Who knows what will happen to us down there. We cannot grow food. A turkey one time a year will not make up for this. Even the laundry crumbles in my hand, with the fumes from your factory. It is a great sacrifice for the men to strike. But maybe you do not know, because you cannot hear over the sound of your parties? The prime minister orders you to a meeting and you will not go? You will not go? Why? Go! Go! Go!

> *Pause.*

SELWYN: Are you done?

> *Pause.*

ANNA: Yes.

SELWYN: Are you quite sure?

ANNA: Yes.

SELWYN: You must be regretting your outburst.

ANNA: I am.

SELWYN: I am sure your family is glad you have the work, now that your brother is no longer capable.

ANNA: We are.

SELWYN: The whole town is in a state. But companies can simply not be run by giving too high a wage to the workers. My bosses would not stand for it. And that is certainly more of an explanation than I owe a housemaid.

Pause. ANNA nods.

STEPHEN: I must go. My train.

GINGER: Thank you for coming.

GINGER helps STEPHEN on with his coat.

SELWYN: This issue must be of some importance to you.

ANNA doesn't know what to say.

SELWYN: Do you absolutely promise to never speak about such things again?

ANNA nods.

STEPHEN: Don't lose heart, my man.

GINGER: I'll try.

Pause. STEPHEN exits.

SELWYN: Do you promise to mend your ways?

ANNA: (*nodding, perhaps holding back tears*) I do.

ACT TWO – Scene Eight
RAILROADED

Smelter WORKERS enter, singing the first part of Earle Peach's "We Cannot Mend Our Ways" (2015).[8]

WORKERS: (*singing*) Whether at the savage rock face or by the smelter grey,
We cannot mend our ways, good gentles,
We cannot mend our ways.
When the factory whistle's shrieking and the lads pour through the gates,
One and all we curse our fates,
We workers, one and all we curse our fates.
For the boss lives in his mansion and with his friends carouses,

---

8   Lyrics and music sheet on next page used with permission.

We Cannot Mend Our Ways

Earle Peach © 2015

Whe-ther at the sa-vage rock face or by the smel-ter grey, we
O the wor-kers of all na-tions con-front a com-mon ill, for the

can-not mend our ways, good gen-tles, we can-not mend our ways. When the
boss does as he will, fel-low wor-kers, the boss does as he will. He

fac-tory whis-tle's shrie-king and the lads pour through the gates, one and
sucks the blood of mil-lions to keep his ban-kers fat, and we've

all we curse our fates, we wor-kers, one and all we curse our fates. For the
had e-nough of that, fel-low wor-kers, we've had quite e-nough of that. For

boss lives in his man-sion and with his friends ca-rou-ses, while the wor-ker must a-
all a-round the world the peo-ple are up-ri-sing, and a new world is now

bide in hum-ble rooms and dank bunk hou-ses. We cre-ate the wealth you
daw-ning through the power of or-ga-ni-zing. We are ma-sters of our

squan-der at the cost of all our days, so we can-not mend our
fu-ture, loo-king for-ward to the day when the wor-kers own the

ways, you bos-ses, we will strike for bet-ter pay.
fac-to-ries and we will sweep you all a-way!

While the worker must abide in humble rooms and dark bunkhouses.
We create the wealth you squander at the cost of all our days,
So we cannot mend our ways,
You bosses, we will strike for better pay.

Lights dim on Selwyn's house. GINGER crosses the stage to the union meeting.

GINGER: Mr. Blaylock, I wanted to be certain that you got the notification of the date and time –

SELWYN: How dare you bother me at my home? How dare you! Don't you be coming around here, threatening me or my family –

GINGER: I'm not, sir.

SELWYN: When my soldier boys are back, they'll take care of the likes of you.

GINGER: Mr. Blaylock, I only wanted to know why –

SELWYN: You'd best watch yourself, Mr. Goodwin. I've had quite enough. I've got influence. I've got connections. And you may not enjoy the results. Now clear out! Clear out!

Lights change. GINGER enters to speak at the union meeting.

GINGER: My brothers and sisters, I have a telegram from the draft board. I am to report for a medical examination.

WORKER 1: But Ginger, you had a medical examination last month.

GINGER: I did. They say they need to re-examine me.

WORKER 7: Why? What's changed?

WORKER 5: The strike. That's what.

WORKER 2: Ginger, you were found unfit.

WORKER 3: Category D.

GINGER: I was.

WORKER 6: The prime minister said there is no way category Ds will be called up.

WORKER 4: We will not have our leaders railroaded to the trenches.

WORKER 8: If Mr. Blaylock and the rest of us can stay out of the war as an essential industry, then you, as our leader, are bloody well essential, too.

WORKER 9: Ginger, we're going to fight this.

GINGER: Thanks, friends. I will appeal in the courts. In the meantime, I believe it's best to follow orders. I'm going to report to the medical officer. I'll be back soon.

GINGER leaves the men and goes to ANNA. She is overcome.

ANNA: Oh, Ginger.

GINGER: It's as I feared, Anna. They are coming after me personally. You could be next.

ANNA: Let us see, let us see what happens. Please?

GINGER looks at ANNA sadly, nods, then exits.

ACT TWO – Scene Nine
ORDERS

GINGER and MEDICAL EXAMINER are at the medical office in Nelson, British Columbia.

MEDICAL EXAMINER: Back again? Orders are orders, eh? *(completely perfunctory, barely giving GINGER a glance)* Open your mouth. Aaaah ... Eyes. Good. No glasses. Squat. Duck walk. Pulse?

GINGER: I still have one.

MEDICAL EXAMINER: Ah, a joker. Let me listen to your heart. Good. Now your lungs. Hmm. Run in place?

GINGER tries to run in place, then has to stop, gasping for breath. It is clear to GINGER that he will die if he's sent to the front lines. He lets the full weight of this hit him.

GINGER: Doctor?

MEDICAL EXAMINER: Yes?

GINGER: I am category D.

MEDICAL EXAMINER: I don't make the final determination.

GINGER: With my black lung, I can't run. And with my ulcer and my digestion, I can't eat, especially army food. I don't believe in shooting another worker –

MEDICAL EXAMINER: Plenty of boys are pacifists. They'll soon train that out of you.

GINGER: Doctor –

MEDICAL EXAMINER: Afraid to meet your maker?

GINGER: I –

MEDICAL EXAMINER: I tell most of the boys to put their affairs in order before they go.

GINGER: Doctor, I won't shoot, can't run, can't eat – I'm afraid to put a fellow soldier at risk.

MEDICAL EXAMINER: Talk to your superior officer. You'll get the results by mail.

ACT TWO – Scene Ten
RESULTS

A transition. GINGER, alone, opens the letter.

GINGER: "Category A. Report for duty."

ACT TWO – Scene Eleven
LEAST

Lights shift. Enters AL (representative from Denver, Colorado, of the International Union of Mine, Mill, and Smelter Workers). GINGER enters, shakes his hand, and gestures for him to sit.

GINGER: Welcome, Al. Mighty fine of you to come up all the way from Denver.

AL: Least I could do. It's a pleasure. From what I hear, they say you're one hell of a strike leader.

GINGER: We're pulling together.

AL: Say, I heard about you being sent to the front lines. Tough break.

GINGER: Yup.

AL: A dirty trick, if you ask me.

GINGER: You're not the only one who thinks so.

AL: I hear your union is fighting it. Don't know much about the appeals in Canada or what not.

GINGER: I appealed at the provincial level – that's like a –

AL: State. Got that. How did it go?

GINGER: Denied. And then the men appealed at the federal level. Denied too. I suppose that might be you next. Now that the US has entered the war.

AL: Yup. I'd be proud to serve. Proud. But I got a bit of a gimpy leg, see?

GINGER: Cause you any pain?

AL: No. But about the war, that's what I've come to see you about.

GINGER: Yes?

AL: Well, there's no easy way to say this.

GINGER: I've been through the worst strikes of the century. You might as well tell me.

AL: Well, you see, you know how we've – I mean the Americans – have entered the war.

GINGER: Yes, been some ten months now, hasn't it?

AL: Yes. Well, you see, since we agreed to sponsor your strike, we unions met with our federal government and, you see, we agreed not to strike for the duration of the war. And that means we can't ... we can't ... you see, even though we are all union brothers, well, it would be against the law for us to give you anything.

> GINGER realizes the strike will have to fold. He is even more distraught.

AL: But you know, I'm sure it's not all for nothing.

> GINGER stands to shake his hand.

GINGER: Thanks for coming up.

AL: Least I could do.

ACT TWO – Scene Twelve
MEND YOUR WAYS

WORKERS and GINGER are meeting at the Union Hall.

WORKER 1: I got this card.

WORKER 2: Me too.

WORKER 1: It's from Mr. Blaylock.

GINGER: (*reading the cards*) "If you promise not to strike for the duration of the war, Mr. Blaylock will hire you back. Sign here, as proof of your promise." Fellows, if you promise not to strike during the war, Mr. Blaylock will take you back on.

WORKER 3: Promise not to strike?

WORKER 4: For the duration of the war?

WORKER 8: Why not for life?

WORKER 5: He's making us promise to mend our ways.

WORKER 6: What power do we have if we can never strike?

WORKER 7: He can do whatever he likes to us, then.

WORKER 9: My notice is different. He says he won't take me back. I'm blacklisted?

GINGER: (*looking at the notice*) It seems so. We'll take this step by step. I'll write to him. Protest this on behalf of the union.

WORKER 1: How can you? You've been sent to the front lines.

GINGER: Brother, I'll send a letter to Mr. Blaylock before I go. My brothers, do not despair. Your bravery will be remembered. One day, and it's not far off, we will have a law that says bosses must abide by the eight-hour day.

WORKER 2: Why's he being sent to war?

WORKER 3: We fought it. All the way to the Supreme Court. We lost.

WORKER 8: Isn't Mr. Blaylock on the draft board?

WORKER 4: He is.

GINGER: My brothers, my sisters, our strike was but one battle in a much bigger war – a war we have waged all over the world, peacefully and bravely, a war we are winning without bullets. It is a war we are winning by downing tools, by refusing to work under their terrible conditions. It is a war we are winning by risking beatings and hunger and blacklists. Our war is the war for the rights of workers. It is my hope that capitalism will fang itself to death, and out of its carcass will spring the life of a new age with blossoms of economic freedom, happiness, and joy for the world's workers. I honour the sacrifices you've made in this strike. It is not all for nothing. Your union brothers and sisters throughout the world thank you. Future generations thank you. For you are fighting not only for the eight-hour day, you are fighting for their lives.

The WORKERS sit in stony silence. Then, slowly, they applaud GINGER and shake his hand.

ACT TWO – Scene Thirteen
RIVER

ANNA is standing at the river, singing a heartbroken song in Italian. GINGER enters. He watches her for a moment. When ANNA sees him, they embrace.

GINGER: You know what I'm here to say, don't you?

ANNA: I do.

GINGER: Anna – it's only a rebel girl like you that made me change my mind and ever think and wish and dream it could be different.

ANNA: I'll wait for you.

GINGER: Anna, I'm about to become public enemy number one.

ANNA: Why?

GINGER: Anna, I didn't report for duty. I am a risk for the other men. I cannot pull my weight in a war. I cannot kill another worker. There's some in Cumberland say they'll help hide me in the wilderness.

ANNA: But the men, they need you. Here. In Trail.

GINGER: Anna. They are trying to dispose of me, by fair means or foul.

ANNA weeps. She holds on to GINGER, who doesn't move.

GINGER: I don't want you to wait. I chose this life.

ANNA: I choose it, too. Let me come with you.

GINGER: It's too dangerous. Anna, they have a posse looking for me. They have orders to capture me, dead or alive. I must go. I want nothing more than to think of you safe and happy and getting on with your life. That will give me strength. Please.

> *They both are unbearably sad. GINGER kisses ANNA goodbye.*

GINGER: Anna, you have my heart.

> *GINGER exits, still holding her red ribbon in his hand.*

ANNA: I am laundry.
I am a shining leaf.
I am a puppy running in the streets.
I am laundry crumbling in the fumes.
I am water filled with chemicals.
I am that puppy dead from poison, by the fall of night.
I am a green leaf turned white, falling apart in your hand.

> *ANNA exits. A guitar plays the melody to "We Cannot Mend Our Ways."*

ACT TWO – Scene Fourteen

IN HIDING

> *GINGER enters, looking for a place to hide. A crack of a twig, and he jumps. It is JOE, who begins singing, to calm GINGER. It's the mid-nineteenth-century traditional northern England song "The Blackleg Miner."*

JOE: (*singing*) It's in the evening after dark,
When the blackleg miner creeps to work,
With his moleskin pants and dirty shirt,
There goes the blackleg miner!

When GINGER recognizes the song, he starts to laugh and sing along. JOE enters with a sack of canned food. GINGER rises to embrace him.

GINGER: Joe.

JOE: Ginger. How's the hideout? Rustic, I see. Food delivered right to thy door. The miners of Cumberland aren't going to let tha starve.

JOE hands GINGER a loaf of bread. GINGER takes the bread and breathes in the smell deeply. Then JOE hands him a fly rod, which GINGER touches reverently.

GINGER: Ta. Cost me a month's pay.

GINGER tries out a few casts.

JOE: Livin' the life out here, blackberries and fresh trout.

GINGER: I'd best not go out. Lest I get shot. But ta.

JOE: Too many bugs the size of Ol' Grimy out there, anyhow.

GINGER: Aye.

A transition. In Trail, RITA leads ANNA by the hand. ANNA is wearing bloomers and a camisole. RITA has a wedding dress over her arm and puts it on ANNA. She gets ANNA up on a table and begins pinning the hem.

RITA: Getting married on a Monday? Is it usual?

ANNA: No. Monday is a laundry day. And I don't want to do laundry for one Monday. At the least.

RITA: Tony Cantafora. He work with your papa?

ANNA: Sì. Mama tried to make the porch nice. Like a parlour. Like rich people. Tony come. He sits. He say nothing. I say nothing. (*pause*) Oh Rita, Ginger asked me to get on with my life. I do not think I can stand.

RITA: You have to.

A transition. Back in Cumberland:

JOE: How's tha holdin' up?

GINGER: Now I know how a deer feels.

JOE: Aye.

GINGER: (*recalling the first lines from Joe Hill's 1915 song "My Last Will"*) But my will is easy to decide ...

JOE: (*completing*) For there is nothing to divide.

GINGER: Aye. (*pause*) If they find me, I'm going to surrender. Rather rot in their jail than die.

A transition. Back in Trail:

RITA: There are not many men to marry anymore. Your family is a lucky to have Tony.

ANNA: What about you, Rita?

RITA: I think I help more as a nurse. If I marry, they make me stop work.

ANNA: Mr. Blaylock fired me when he found out I was getting married.

RITA: Married ladies are supposed to work only for family.

A transition. In Cumberland:

JOE: Oh Ginger. Maybe I should have never asked tha to agitate with me. Maybe I should have never started talkin' hope to thee. I've asked tha to risk too much.

GINGER: Joe, I should be dead for a thousand reasons. A mine collapse, an explosion. A soldier beating me down in a strike. Hunger. Me lungs. Anything. Without you, Joe, it would be my destiny to dig the rich man's coal. That's all. To rank below the mules.

JOE: And what do you suppose your destiny is now?

GINGER: Will I be remembered, you mean?

JOE: Aye.

A transition. In Trail:

ANNA: I still have job at hotel. No one there cares what I do.

RITA: That is lucky. Ha. Because nobody want to do laundry.

ANNA: Right. Nobody want to do. Sì. Rita, do you not want to have children?

RITA: I could not bear to send them to war.

ANNA: I would teach a baby how to make a better life.

RITA: Like Ginger?

ANNA: (*nodding*) Sì. And I'd name him Luigi.

A transition. In Cumberland:

GINGER: I hope to live.

JOE: 'Course.

GINGER: But if I don't –

JOE: Aye.

GINGER: If I have to be remembered, 'stead of alive ...

JOE: Aye?

GINGER: I hope to be remembered –

JOE: Aye –

GINGER: When things get terribly tough –

JOE: Like they are now –

GINGER: When it all seems hopeless.

JOE: Why on earth do you want to be remembered in a terrible time?

GINGER: Because that's when it matters most. I want to be remembered when a worker reaches out to help a fellow worker.

JOE: Aye.

GINGER: When a worker says, "We're in this together, we can do better." Like you did for me.

JOE: Aye. Tha will be.

> *GINGER and JOE embrace, as if they know it is the last time they'll see each other. JOE claps GINGER on a shoulder, exits.*

A transition. In Trail:

RITA: You look beautiful. Like hope.

ANNA, heartbroken, smiles at RITA.

ANNA: Grazie.

ACT TWO – Scene Fifteen
I REMAIN

GINGER, alone. He hears the branches crack and believes the posse has come for him. He grabs a pen and writes.

MARY ANN enters, carrying Ginger's journal, which has a red ribbon tucked in its pages.

The reading of the following letter is divided between GINGER and MARY ANN.

MARY ANN / GINGER: (*reading*) "Dear Mum. Now they are upon me, I hear the branches crack. It's time I must surrender. It would do no good to run. I would rather face a prison term than a bounty hunter's gun. I remain your affectionate son …"

GINGER rises, steps outside the cabin, and raises his hands in surrender. The crack of a gun. GINGER falls to the ground.

POSTLUDE

WORKER 1: (*singing from "The Day They Shot Ginger Down"*) It was a
black day for Cumberland, a black day for the miners ...
The day they shot Ginger down.

WORKER: (*speaking*) When they shot him down, we downed tools
across the city.

WORKER: It was Vancouver's first general strike.

WORKER: When they shot him down, we downed tools across
the country.

WORKER: It was Canada's first general strike.

WORKER: And the eight-hour day became law.

    Then all WORKERS sing "We Cannot Mend our Ways."

WORKERS: Whether at the savage rock face or by the smelter grey,
We cannot mend our ways, good gentles,
We cannot mend our ways.
When the factory whistle's shrieking and the lads pour through the gates,
One and all we curse our fates,
We workers, one and all we curse our fates.
For the boss lives in his mansion and with his friends carouses,
While the worker must abide in humble rooms and dark bunkhouses.
We create the wealth you squander at the cost of all our days,
So we cannot mend our ways,
You bosses, we will strike for better pay.
O the workers of all nations confront a common ill,
For the boss does as he will,
Fellow workers, the boss does as he will.
He sucks the blood of millions to keep his bankers fat,
And we've had enough of that, fellow workers,
We've had quite enough of that.
For all around the world
The people are uprising, and a new world is now dawning
Through the power of organizing.
We are masters of future, looking forward to the day
When the workers own the factories and we will sweep you all away!

    The End

ACKNOWLEDGMENTS

for The Ballad of Ginger Goodwin

Special Thanks: Charles Simard, Kevin and Vicki Williams, Talonbooks, Kathleen Weiss, Kathleen Flaherty, Heidi Taylor, Playwrights Theatre Centre, Beth Leonard, Western Washington University Theatre Arts, Gary Cristall, Bill Clark, Juno Ávila-Clark, Earle Peach, Judy Fraser, Lorae Farrell, Cumberland Museum and Archives, Bill Clark Sr., Gwen Clark, Kamarie Chapman, and Wayde Compton.

KITIMAT

To the citizens of Kitimat

and

to my Azorean great-grandfather
António Garcia Porto who was lost at sea

FROM THE AZORES TO THE ANTHROPOCENE

Place and Time in Elaine Ávila's Kitimat

Along with the characters, dialogues, and settings that breathe life into a stage production, place and time are key players in Elaine Ávila's *Kitimat*. In English the usual sequence is "time and place," but in this play, as in the title above, "place" takes precedence. First, the play is named for and set in the British Columbian port town of Kitimat, a name derived from "Git-a-maat" or "Kitamaat," the Ts'msyen term that designates the x̄á'isla (Haisla) inhabitants of the region as "people of the snow." In tandem with depicting this place "of the snow," *Kitimat* is about the impact of immigration, the dramatic move from one place to another that happens when the first generation takes the leap and migrates, setting in motion a series of unknown outcomes for their descendants. In this case, the immigrants are from the Azores Islands and their destination was the town of Kitimat, on the western coast of Canada, halfway between the US states of Washington and Alaska, a leap of thousands of kilometres for the Azoreans who settled in this region.

Place also comes first precisely because *Kitimat* is a play centred on immigration from the Azores, a nine-island archipelago situated in the middle of the North Atlantic that was discovered by the Portuguese in 1432. Politically, the Azorean archipelago is today an autonomous region of Portugal and an outermost region of the European Union, making it the westernmost point of Europe. Geologically, these volcanic islands, the summits of the Mid-Atlantic Ridge that runs north–south along the floor of the Atlantic Ocean, are spread over the junction of three tectonic plates – the Eurasian, the African, and the North American Plates. Culturally, the people of the Azores have been indelibly shaped and reshaped by this oceanic location and volcanic situation. Perhaps the most eloquent yet simple definition of Azorean reality was formulated by our most renowned writer, Vitorino Nemésio, when he wrote (in his 1932 book *Sob os signos de agora*)[9] that, to Azoreans, "geography is as important as history." Within this setting, Nemésio also wrote, and I paraphrase, that since we are rooted by our habitat to mountains of lava, we are made of flesh and stones; our bones are submerged in the sea, which Nemésio sees as foundational and essential.

As this key role of geography unfolds onstage, history and time are also

---

9   Vitorino Nemésio, *Sob os signos de agora: Temas portugueses e brasileiros* (Coimbra, Portugal: Imprensa da Universidade, 1932).

fundamental to the structure and action of *Kitimat*. Within the temporal scenario, Elaine Ávila takes us back to the early 1950s, when historians agree that Azoreans began to immigrate to Canada. Indeed, within the geography and history of Portuguese immigration to North America, 1953 has been officially pinpointed as the year when the first group of eighteen islanders boarded a ship in the port of Ponta Delgada, hoping to make a new life for themselves in Canada. Other individuals had taken the leap before, however. Among these was Pedro da Silva (1647–1717), the Portuguese immigrant who was identified as the "first courier in New France" by Canada Post, which issued an official stamp in 2003 in his honour and in celebration of the fiftieth anniversary of Portuguese immigration to Canada. Yet another significant situation happened during the cod-fishing expeditions that took place yearly up until the early 1950s. These were transatlantic expeditions during which more than three thousand Portuguese fishermen, including Azoreans, lost their lives in Canadian waters. Those whose bodies were retrieved were usually buried in Catholic cemeteries in St. John's, Newfoundland and Labrador. During this same time period, but on the West Coast, outsiders began to arrive and settle in British Columbia's Kitimat region, which had been inhabited by the Nations of the x̄á'isla and neighbouring Ts'msyen for millennia. Following suit, Azoreans began to make their way to the town of Kitimat, where they would, according to Elaine in an interview, come to comprise 50 percent of the population; in act one, scene seventeen, one of the play's choristers says they were 40 percent in 1958.

In this context, *Kitimat* takes us back to the 1950s and the mixture of pain and hope underlying the immigrants' situation, here depicted by José and Clara da Terra ("da terra," literally "from the land, the place of origin" in Portuguese). Throughout the play, this earlier time period is intertwined with the lives of the da Terra offspring and their children up to 2014, the year of the historic plebiscite on the proposed construction of a massive network of pipelines reaching Kitimat. This time frame is fundamental to the storyline of the play, of course, but it also happens to coincide with the period during which environmental issues and problems came to occupy centre stage in our society. In fact, from the mid-1900s, especially from the 1960s, to the early 2000s, efforts have been made to increase environmental awareness and protection, with dramatically inchoate and incipient results, while environmental degradation has snowballed. Indeed, the momentum and importance of the environmental movement of this period have been such that scientists were prompted to name our geological era as the Anthropocene, the era when *anthrōpoi* ("humans" in Greek) have so impacted life on this planet that they had the inauspicious honour of having a geological epoch named after them.

In sum, this is the timespan depicted in *Kitimat* – the period of time when three generations of immigrants develop and interact, the second recalling the first, and the third looking ahead, with more or less hope, depending on their circumstances. Doubt seems to prevail in the younger generation, as evoked, in act one, scene three, in the exchange between Clara and José's two grandchildren. Ana, the granddaughter, proposes, "Let's toast to Grandma. And Grandpa ... To José and Clara. To the dreams of the past," to which her cousin Nuno retorts, "Why? Because there are no dreams of the future?" As they click their beer bottles in a toast, Ana replies, ambiguously, with the rhetorical question, "Who knows?"

Simultaneously, the temporality of the play can also be said to correlate with the time it took the scientific community to develop the concept of the Anthropocene, as notions about ecology and the dynamics of life on this planet emerged from the second half of the twentieth century, merging into the new century and new millennium. This movement would converge more ominously in our time and become the driving force behind the playwright's concerns – raising environmental awareness and taking action in the Anthropocene.

In many ways, Julia Viveiros – José and Clara's youngest daughter, married to Manny Viveiros – is the pivotal character of the play, as she moves from cherishing her mother's memories of the Azores to defending her hometown, Kitimat, from the environmental threat posed by the projected pipeline. Overall, this is an experiential trajectory that takes her, both metaphorically and existentially, from the Azores to the Anthropocene, from a place of memories and saudade to a time of environmental crisis and action. In the end, although it is Julia's daughter, Ana, and her nephew Nuno, representing the younger generation, who plan to leave for college in order to further their education, Julia is the one who develops the social skills and environmental literacy required to participate in the campaign for the "no" vote in the play's 2014 plebiscite, thereby reversing her past situation. Indeed, years before, Julia had stayed home to take care of her aging parents while her older sister Marta had left for college and become the first woman in the family to receive a university degree. With Julia's new-found personal awareness and activism in her community, the "no" was eventually successful in stopping the pipeline construction project, an ecological and environmental threat to the natural coastline of BC's North Coast. To this day, Kitimat remains the only BC municipality to have held a referendum on the controversial Pacific Northern Gas Pacific Trail Pipeline and Enbridge Northern Gateway Pipelines.

All things considered, the tension between the two da Terra sisters seems to lend feminist contours to the play. As an activist, Julia is pitted against her older sister Marta, a real-estate broker and city councillor who is an avid supporter of the multi-billion-dollar pipeline project. The play opens with the family gathered for Marta's birthday. Julia, true to her role of caregiver, brings the pineapple cake she made from their mother's secret recipe, a specialty of the islands. True also to her Azorean roots, Julia speaks with longing sadness and saudade about her deceased parents, especially her mother Clara, who left her the statue of Mary that she cherishes and prays to in times of need. In keeping with this feminine dynamic, Julia's great ally in the campaign against the pipeline is Barb, a nurse and amateur naturalist who helped Julia take care of her aging parents. In answer to Marta's sardonic question in act two, scene three, "How long have you known these nature people?," Julia underscores the personal nature of her relationship with Barb and, by extension, with her fellow activists, when she replies, "Barb was Mom's nurse," succinctly putting her sister in her place.

In the end, Julia's awakening to environmental protection and action can be seen as an extension of her role as caregiver, protecting nature as she protected her parents and the Azorean immigrant legacy they left her. This combination of her Azorean roots and environmental activism seem to come to full fruition in act two, scene twenty-three, as *Kitimat* approaches its conclusion and Julia's husband Manny urges her to go watch the results of the voting with her fellow activists. Touched by his empathy and support, Julia replies affectionately, "I love you. You stand by me when it matters most." In a response that, in essence, connects the Azores to the Anthropocene, Manny speaks for the last time and says: "Julia, you've found a beautiful way to honour José and Clara's memory. You have. Now go! Find out how everyone voted!"

—**ROSA MARIA NEVES SIMAS**

Ponta Delgada, Azores

August 10, 2022

The eyes of the future are looking back at us and they are praying for us to be able to see beyond our own time.

—TERRY TEMPEST WILLIAMS

Refuge: An Unnatural History of Family and Place (1991)

Like all those who emigrate, my parents started a family as if it were a country. Like all emigrants, they told stories. But these were not just stories. They were ships, they were journeys, they were return trips home.

—MIA COUTO

"When Did I Become a Writer?" (2014), trans. Zoë Perry

We exist. We are here. We are entitled to poetry.

—MIGDALIA CRUZ

in Brian Eugenio Herrera, *The Latino|a Theatre Commons 2013 National Convening: A Narrative Report* (2015)

PRODUCTION HISTORY

Kitimat was commissioned by the Mellon Elemental Arts Initiative at Pomona College's Departments of Theatre and Dance and first produced at the Seaver Theatre in Claremont, California, from April 9 to 12, 2015, with the following cast and crew:

JULIA – Sarah Lopez
MANNY – Robert Larsen
ANA – Allegra Cox
MARTA – Katia Mafra Spencer
NUNO – Peter Atkin
JIMMY – Henry Colt
BARB – Elvia Espinoza
TIM – Peter Lane
CLARA – Maroon Stranger
JOSÉ – Juan Zamudio
CHORUS – Anna Dowling, Nyia Hamilton, Peter Lane, Milagros Montalvo, Simone Nibbs, Kirsten Tingle

Director – Janet Hayatshahi
Assistant Director – Kat Milukas
Dramaturge – Isabel Semler
Set Designer – Christopher Scott Murillo
Costume Designer – Sherry Linnell
Lighting Designer – Sherrice Mojgan
Sound Designer – Nicholas Drashner
Stage Manager – Michelle Chesley
Assistant Stage Manager – Dixinyao (Moonlight) Zhu

This play was supported by the Associates program of the Playwrights Theatre Centre (PTC) in Vancouver, British Columbia.

CAST

2013–2014 period

JULIA Viveiros, fifty-three, a receptionist at the real-estate office

MANNY Viveiros, fifty-six, Julia's husband and worker at the smelter

ANA, twenty, Julia and Manny's daughter and a supervisor at Kitimat's
  Ol' Keg Pub

MARTA, fifty-six, Julia's sister and a real-estate broker and city councillor

NUNO, twenty-two, Marta's son and an insulator at the smelter

JIMMY, twenty-three, an out-of-town welder

BARB, forty-four, a nurse and amateur naturalist

TIM, twenty-six, a canvasser for the oil company

1957–1958 period

CLARA da Terra, twenty, and JOSÉ da Terra, twenty-two: two recently
married immigrants to Kitimat from the Azores, an autonomous region
of Portugal in the Atlantic Ocean.

Both periods

The CHORUS: In act one, they are founders and first residents from the
1950s, with a few exceptions. In act two, they are people from 2014: city
planners, filmmakers, reporters, residents, Azoreans, members of the x̌á'isla
(Haisla) Nation, employees of the oil company, or members of a grassroots
environmental group.

Note on distribution

Kitimat can use a flexible cast size, between six and sixteen actors. For
a cast of six, for example, double roles could be as follows: Clara/Ana,
Jimmy/Tim, and Marta/Barb; or Marta/Clara, Ana/Barb, and Nuno/Tim.
Chorus members can be played by all actors. It is strongly preferred that
actors of all ethnicities and genders play these roles. Due to a large dias-
pora, Azoreans are often mixed-race – Inuit, xʷməθkʷəẏəm, Moroccan,
South Asian, Latinx, African, Asian … X̄á'isla activist and advisor Nancy
Nyce has given her permission for her direct quote to be used in act one,
scene eleven. Although in the original production, this line was spoken by
a non-Indigenous actor, every effort should be made to cast Indigenous
actors.

TIME

From June 2013 to April 2014 for the first time frame, and from 1952 to 1958 for the second (see the character list above)

PLACE

Kitimat, British Columbia

SETTING

The remains of a worn-down, mid-century modern industrial town is carved out of a misty and beautiful wilderness. A few set pieces establish the Viveiroses' home and the various locales around the city. At minimum, these are:

a sofa and a chair, both covered in plastic

a double bed

a bedside table with an altar

a dining room table with five chairs

Other places referred to in the play can be brought onstage through the actors' performances and using minimal props.

PLAYWRIGHT'S NOTE

Although it is inspired by true events and informed by interviews, *Kitimat* is a work of fiction. All of the characters, organizations, and events portrayed in this play are either products of the author's imagination or are employed fictitiously.

Special thanks to Nancy Nyce for permission to quote her in the play.

At the urging of Marta (Katia Mafra Spencer), Julia (Sarah Lopez) models her mother's shoes, one of the first signs of Clara's achievement as an immigrant and of the family's rise out of poverty.
Photo: Carrie Rosema, courtesy of Pomona College

Clara (Maroon Stranger) begs her new husband, José (Juan Zamudio), to trust her and describe the dangers of working in the smelter.
Photo: Carrie Rosema, courtesy of Pomona College

PROLOGUE

*January 2014. We first hear the natural sounds of the
municipality of Kitimat – wind, water, birds. Then come
industrial sounds – the smelter, construction, trucks.*

*JULIA enters with an old suitcase. She opens it, but is quickly
overcome with emotion. She shuts the case and speaks to the
audience.*

JULIA: I'm Julia. I live in a town that's nearly dying, that you've never
heard of, deep in the wilderness, near Alaska, a Canadian utopia.
Kitimat. (*beat*) We make the aluminum that fills this theatre. We make
electricity that lights this stage.[10] Last year, in Kitimat, we nearly came
apart – we were asked to vote. (*beat*) To tell you, I need my mother.
My father. They're dead now, but this is how I remember them.

CLARA and JOSÉ enter as JULIA names them.

My friend, my sister, my daughter, my nephew, my husband.

BARB, MARTA, ANA, NUNO, and MANNY enter.

Kitimat.

---

10 Playwright's note: This is true for a significant portion of Western Canada and the West
Coast of the United States. If producing this play in another region, feel free to adapt
the line accordingly.

ACT ONE – Scene One

The Viveiros home, January 2014. MARTA is seated at the dining room table, with MANNY, ANA, and NUNO. JULIA enters, carrying a cake.

MARTA: Bolo de ananas?[11] Julia, how did you get Mom to give you the recipe?

JULIA: I have my ways.

MARTA starts to get tears in her eyes.

MARTA: I thought I'd never taste her cake again.

JULIA: (*smiling*) Nothing is too good for my sister. Congratulations.

MANNY: Congratulations, Marta.

NUNO: Way to go, Mom.

ANA: Congratulations, Auntie Marta!

JULIA cuts the cake and hands it out.

JULIA: To Marta.

NUNO: Approved by the National Energy Board.

ALL: To Marta.

Everyone toasts MARTA with their cake.

MARTA: Thanks everybody. (*pause*) Julia, you … you went kayaking?

JULIA: Why is that so hard to believe?

ANA: You're not the outdoors-type mom.

JULIA: What? I'm scared of bears.

Everyone laughs.

JULIA: The whales have come back. From what we've done to them. In record numbers. They love to sing in our channel, they love the echoes.

MARTA: "From what we've done to them"?

JULIA: They've recovered. From industry.

---

11 Pineapple cake [an Azorean classic].

MARTA: Excuse me?

JULIA: I went kayaking with Barb. We saw a whale breach, right in front of us.

MARTA: Oh my god. I would freak out.

JULIA: I saw into the whale's eye. I remembered how Dad and his friends would go out in canoes and harpoon whales, back in Portugal. Whales used to feed our families. Their bones, their teeth became part of our guitars, our clothes, the toys for the children. Their oil went into the lamps at night, so we could read and sew and knit. We're alive because of them. (*beat*) A whale. That close.

MARTA: Barb. You were kayaking with Barb?

JULIA: Yes.

MARTA: One of Mom's nurses.

JULIA: Right.

MARTA: She's one of the nature people, the political people.

JULIA crosses back to the dinner table while BARB exits.

JULIA: I like to get out. Now that I can.

ANA: What's the big deal?

NUNO: The whale people are concerned about the pipeline. That the supertankers will scare the whales away.

ANA: Oh.

NUNO: Plus the effects of a spill –

MARTA: Potential spill.

NUNO: Right.

MARTA: Julia, how much are you and Barb hanging out?

JULIA: I don't talk politics with her.

MARTA: Querida,[12] you know the cost.

JULIA: I do.

MARTA: Where's the map? The one that was on the wall?

JULIA: Mom panicked.

---

12 Darling.

ANA: It made her so upset.

MARTA: Why?

ANA: All the places she'd never see.

MARTA: God rest her soul.

ANA: Can we finally get rid of some of their stuff?

JULIA: I –

ANA: When will you? It's been a year.

MANNY: Leave your mother alone.

MARTA: Why don't you get your own place?

ANA: Can't afford it. Rents too high. Zero vacancy.

MARTA: Julia, tell you what: I'll help you. Go through their things.

ANA: Thank you, Aunt Marta.

MARTA: You're welcome.

NUNO: My truck is awesome.

> *ANA groans and socks NUNO in the arm.*

ANA: We know.

NUNO: What? It is.

MANNY: Can you get it up the mountains?

NUNO: Easy.

MANNY: Never gets stuck?

NUNO: Never.

JULIA: More cake?

> *JULIA offers everyone more cake, but they shake their heads no.*
> *The guests begin gathering their coats and aiming for the door.*

JULIA: (*to the audience*) But this story began when Kitimat was founded, over sixty years ago, and it isn't only about my family.

> *ALL family members exit except JULIA, who lingers a*
> *moment, watching two CHORUS members rise from the*
> *audience.*

CHORISTER 1: Nineteen fifty-two.

CHORISTER 2: Kitimat is only a twinkle in the industry's eye.

JULIA exits.

ACT ONE – Scene Two

Kitimat, 1952. CHORUS members as actors perform an advertisement from the 1950s.

CHORISTER 1: It will be a test of human intelligence and strength.

CHORISTER 2: To build the largest aluminum smelter in the world.

CHORISTER 3: This will be bigger than finishing the railway.

CHORISTER 4: It will open up Canada.

CHORISTER 5: Make profits and generate electricity for generations.

CHORISTER 6: Save the masses from the slums of Europe.

CHORISTER 5: We'll blow up a mountain.

CHORISTER 6: Scoop it into a dam.

CHORISTER 1: Make ourselves a lake.

CHORISTER 2: Make a river flow backwards.

CHORISTER 3: Secure the rights to land, sea, and river.

CHORISTER 4: Build a whale of a hydroelectric plant.

CHORISTER 5: Sixteen times the height of Niagara Falls.

CHORISTER 6: We'll need workers.

CHORISTER 2: We'll make a great place to live.

CHORISTER 3: We'll get the best town planners in the world.

CHORISTER 4: From New York.

CHORISTER 5: Make tomorrow's city today.

CHORISTER 6: Unique in all of North America.

CHORISTER 5: Build everything in two and half years.

CHORISTER 6: Every month of delay would be a loss of millions of dollars of profit.

CHORISTER 1: We'll call it Kitimat: City of the Future.

ACT ONE – Scene Three

Outside Kitimat's Ol' Keg Pub, January 2014. ANA is looking at the sky. NUNO has been drinking.

ANA: You can see lots of stars –

NUNO: In the middle of nowhere.

ANA: It's beautiful.

NUNO: What's a Kitimat suitcase?

ANA: Come on, Nuno ... that joke ... it's so old.

NUNO: What's a Kitimat suitcase?

ANA: You know I hate that joke.

NUNO: A two-four.

ANA: Ha ha. A two-four. Why don't we just say "twenty-four cans of beer"?

NUNO: Because "two-four" sounds cool.

ANA: I actually don't get it.

NUNO: I know you don't.

ANA: It's stupid. So what? People drink. In Kitimat. They drink a lot. Ha ha.

NUNO: Sometimes it's the only way to get out.

ANA: Stupid. Is that what we're known for? "Kitimat, People of Beer." Wow. I'm so proud.

NUNO: (*laughing*) Kitimat suitcase. Never gets old.

ANA: Dude. It is so *old*. I work in a bar. How many times do you think I've heard that joke?

NUNO: I don't like you working there. Those guys, they are so sleazy.

ANA: Not all of them.

NUNO: Most of them.

ANA: (*laughing*) Most of them. I can handle myself. Guess what? I've been promoted. You're looking at a shift manager.

NUNO: Congratulations.

ANA: Thanks. I still make one tenth of what you do.

NUNO: It was awesome that you helped with Grandma.

ANA: It was some of the best moments of my life.

NUNO: C'mon. She was pretty sick. It must have been pretty –

ANA: Yup. It was rough. But I got to be with her.

NUNO: Now that Grandma's … passed, you could do anything.

ANA: I don't want to be exported. Even though that's what we were raised for.

NUNO: All our friends are gone.

ANA: And your dad.

NUNO: Him too.

ANA: How is he?

NUNO: No idea.

ANA: You don't hear anything from him?

NUNO: Nope. He totally lost it. They always talk about how resilient we are in Kitimat, through booms and busts, isolation and winter. Whatever. Not all of us.

ANA: That sucks. Poor Aunt Marta.

NUNO: She's fine. Let's toast to my new truck.

ANA: Not again.

NUNO: To my new truck. It has –

ANA: I know, I know, it's the best truck ever built.

NUNO: It is.

ANA: It can go anywhere, handle anything.

NUNO: Mud –

ANA: The thickest mud.

NUNO: Snow –

ANA: The iciest. I know, it's totally rad.

NUNO: It is. If I hit a deer, I won't die.

ANA: I'll drink to that.

> *NUNO hands ANA a beer.*

ANA: I'm freezing.

NUNO: We could go somewhere.

ANA: Where?

NUNO: Exactly.

ANA: Let's toast to Grandma. And Grandpa.

NUNO: Okay.

ANA: To José and Clara. To the dreams of the past.

NUNO: Why? Because there are no dreams of the future?

ANA: Who knows?

> *NUNO clinks his beer bottle with ANA's, and they drink.*

ACT ONE – Scene Four

> *The da Terra living room, 1958. JOSÉ and CLARA enter.*
> *We hear late 1950s music scratching on a phonograph,[13]*
> *distorted through the lens of memory – a sound cue occurring*
> *every time JOSÉ and CLARA enter a scene. JOSÉ sets down*
> *CLARA's suitcase and turns to her.*

JOSÉ: Close your eyes.

> *CLARA closes her eyes. JOSÉ leads her in.*

JOSÉ: Open.

> *CLARA surveys her new home.*

CLARA: Oh, José.

JOSÉ: You like?

CLARA: I love it. Is it all for us only?

JOSÉ: (*nodding*) Yes.

---

13 Music suggestions: instrumentals openings by Amália Rodrigues, Lawrence Welk, Dean
Martin, Dinah Washington ...

CLARA: Oh José, it is very grand. It comes with furniture?

JOSÉ: Yes. From the company. Yes. The smelter.

CLARA: Did you ever think you would ever have such a house?

JOSÉ: Never in all my life. When that man catcher – that's what they called the guy who comes to talk to us in Montréal, in the work camp. The man catcher –

CLARA: (*intrigued, awkwardly practising one of her first English terms*) Man catcher.

JOSÉ: When he came, he said we could have a house, a family. Imagine. I had no home. Everything was work camp to work camp. Sending money back to my parents in the Azores. And here he comes, saying we could have a family, a future. And he told the truth. The dream. Here it is. Running water, right in the house. You just turn. (*as if turning the tap on*) And such nice beds. And electricity, light, with just a close and open of this on the wall. (*as if flicking a light switch on and off*) And machines to keep food cold: in English, they call it "refrigerator."

CLARA: A – what? A – rator? A rator.

JOSÉ: Refrigerator.

> *CLARA tries to say "refrigerator" but can't and begins laughing.*

JOSÉ: I went down to the company dock with all the others and there were hundreds of them. For all of us. Hundreds.

CLARA: One for everybody.

JOSÉ: And places for us to take the English classes in the nights. All provided.

CLARA: I can learn.

JOSÉ: The dream. And here you are. Here we are.

CLARA: Married.

JOSÉ: Even though we had never met.

CLARA: It was the wish – the need of my parents. It is a long way.

JOSÉ: I understand. I agree.

CLARA: Where did you take your vows?

JOSÉ: All we have for a church in Kitimat is a little shack we call Joey, but it is where we go.

CLARA: The Joey Shack?

JOSÉ: Like Portuguese Joe, Portuguese John, Portuguese José. All the English guys think our first name is Portuguese.

CLARA: The Portuguese Joey Shack.

JOSÉ: Yes, it is our church. So I stepped into the Joey Shack, on Sunday, May 23, 1958. Ten in the morning, Kitimat time. And you stepped in the church, at the same time as me –

CLARA: Five in the afternoon in the Azores. It is strange. I know. My father's idea.

JOSÉ: I never imagined I'd be alone. At the altar. (*taking out a small photograph*) All I had was this little photograph of you.

CLARA: (*also taking out a small photograph*) All I had was this little photograph of you. (*starting to cry*) Oh, José.

JOSÉ: Why are you sad? Tell me.

CLARA: My sisters, my friends –

JOSÉ: You miss them? Don't be afraid. Here is a free country. You can speak. Without fear.

> *JULIA enters and watches CLARA and JOSÉ from afar. They do not see her.*

CLARA: They cannot get permission from Salazar to leave, like us. Is very hard there now. My little brother, he spoke badly about him. One word against Salazar, one time: they locked him up, who knows, for forever. And they take all the young men of our village for the wars in Angola. When they come back – they – they –

JOSÉ: I know. They are not themselves.

CLARA: I try to not think of sad things. Happy things tonight. You know, if we can speak, freely, we are in a kind of heaven. On my, I mean our, wedding day, with the money you sent, we made a delicious cake, and I rented a beautiful dress.

*CHORUS members enter as villagers from the Azores. They
play music and dance the Azorean chamarrita.*[14]

CLARA: All the village came, the church was filled. We had a huge party
with food, and music, and dancing. My sisters, my friends were all
there. I gave them a piece of wedding cake so they could put it under
their bed and dream of someone to marry them, too.

> *The CHORUS dances off and exits. JULIA exits with the
> CHORUS.*

JOSÉ: May I kiss you?

> *CLARA nods, nervously. They kiss their first kiss. It is
> awkward. JOSÉ takes her suitcase to the bedroom. Not sure
> what to do, CLARA follows him. She lies down on the bed,
> with all her clothes on, extremely nervous. He sighs, lies down
> on the bed, with all his clothes on. They stare into space,
> worried that their marriage won't work and unsure what to
> do.*

ACT ONE – Scene Five

> *In the District of Kitimat City Council's meeting room and
> in the Viveiros home's living room, January 2014. MARTA,
> in the middle of the audience, is making a televised speech
> to city council. In parallel, JULIA enters her living room and
> turns on the TV to watch MARTA's speech. Light falls across
> JULIA's face. The CHORUS also enters JULIA's living room
> and watches, as if all are watching from their private TVs.*

MARTA: Seven years ago, we thought Kitimat would die. Like many of
you, my husband and I got laid off when the pulp mill closed. And
then ... (*with tears welling up in her eyes*) we almost lost our home.
It was worth nothing. We had no one to sell it to. No – we were
screwed. A bust, an economic downturn – I don't have to tell you –
it leads to depression, drinking, divorce. Your friends, your family
move away. (*pause, almost weeping again, then taking a breath*) But all
that's changed. We've done it. We're in a boom. Our houses are worth
three times what they were worth last year. We wooed industry back

---

14 Playwright's note: I am descended from the Azorean island of Pico, so I'm thinking
here of the chamarrita of Pico. But the Viveiroses are from Achadinha, on the island
of São Miguel, which has its own chamarrita. There are many YouTube videos showing
different chamarritas: you are welcome to use the one you like best.

to Kitimat. The mayor, the former mayor, and the council should all be congratulated. Instead, we hear, meeting after meeting, from people wanting us to take a stand against the pipeline. (*scoffing*) We hear that we are the only city council in the north that supports this project. Okay. What do we do? (*pause, then a sudden inspiration*) Let's put it to a vote. I call for a plebiscite. Let Kitimat decide.

JULIA is shocked.

ACT ONE – Scene Six

Kitimat, 1953. CHORUS members enter as city planners. They are making this up as they go along.

CHORISTER 1: Kitimat has much to contend with.

CHORISTER 2: Climate.

CHORISTER 3: Remoteness and …

CHORISTER 4: Strangeness.

CHORISTER 5: Nearest village is seven kilometres away.

CHORISTER 1: And it's just the First Nations. The x̄á'isla.

CHORISTER 2: Who?

CHORISTER 1: The x̄á'isla.

CHORUS members try to pronounce "x̄á'isla" (a.k.a. "Haisla") with difficulty.[15] CHORISTER 1 attempts to correct them, fairly unsuccessfully.

CHORISTER 4: But the town site for Kitimat –

CHORISTER 5: Uninhabited. A completely blank slate.

CHORISTER 3: Except for mud and trees.

CHORISTER 6: Sixty-six square miles.

---

15 For an accurate pronunciation of the x̄á'isla (Haisla) ethnonym, interested readers can watch the following YouTube Short by Teresa Windsor, a First Nations speaker of X̄a'islak̓ala: "Xaisla is a 3-syllable word," posted by Haisla Kala, August 10, 2018, youtube.com/shorts/v8e4wez01NA. To hear the word spoken by two x̄á'isla Elders, see this YouTube video: "FNEF presents Rapid Word Collection with Haislakala," posted by the First Nations Education Foundation, April 12, 2021, starting at 6:53 ("Sounds, Pronunciation & Sharing"), youtu.be/d2lY3T0hUw4?t=413.

CHORISTER 3: The setting for a good life must be hewn out of unknown wilderness.

CHORISTER 4: I'm concerned about loneliness. The monotony of a one-industry town. It could lead to broken marriages, rough housing. General disquiet.

CHORISTER 5: Pioneers must become old-timers, bound to Kitimat by their love of the town and its unusual qualities.

ALL exit.

ACT ONE – Scene Seven

BARB's place in Kitimat, January 2014. JULIA and BARB are having tea.

JULIA: Why am I so angry?

BARB: She suffered.

JULIA: Why did she get so sick? Because of the smelter? The pulp mill?

BARB: Hard to prove.

JULIA: What about Dad? Safety standards were so low back then.

BARB: Lots of cancer here.

JULIA: Will I ever be able to stop?

BARB: What?

JULIA: Mourning?

BARB: Maybe not. But you'll find a beautiful way to honour their memories. You will.

JULIA: Have you found that for Bob?

BARB: Not yet. It still hurts.

JULIA: What was it again?

BARB: Lung cancer.

JULIA: How awful.

BARB: We had twenty good years.

JULIA: You did.

BARB pours JULIA some tea. JULIA notices two glossy reports on the table.

JULIA: What's that?

BARB: The *National Energy Board Report.*

JULIA: Wow. It's thick. Can I look at it?

BARB: Be my guest. I don't know what I expected. Santa Claus? The National Energy Board is three people with close ties to the oil industry. Of course they approved the pipeline. I don't think they listened to us. Or the scientists. Or the x̄á'isla.

JULIA: The x̄á'isla. They're against it, right?

BARB: Right. And now, this plebiscite.

JULIA: The one my sister called for?

BARB: Yes. Every other city council in the north is officially against it – but ours. They won't take a stand until they see how the voters of Kitimat feel. It's a free public-opinion poll.

JULIA: For city councillors.... So they can get re-elected. And for the pipeline company. Who pays for a plebiscite?

BARB: We do.

JULIA: Wow.

JULIA flips through the report, stunned.

ACT ONE – Scene Eight

Kitimat's Hospital Beach, near the smelter, January 2014. ANA and NUNO are sitting on a log or stone bench, finishing two bottles of beer.

ANA: Was your mom seriously part of approving Kitimat's first escort agency?

NUNO: (*nodding, then imitating his mother*) "It's good business. Young men have needs. I, for one, don't want all the out-of-town construction workers preying on our daughters."

ANA: Have you used them?

NUNO: Who?

ANA: Dude, don't play dumb. The escort service.

NUNO: Yeah.

ANA: What was it like?

NUNO: Great.

ANA: Really? You can tell me. What was she like?

NUNO: It's better with a girlfriend. Why don't you ask me about my truck?

ANA: Do you like it better than her?

NUNO: The truck is amazing, Ana. I can make it to all the towns of the north whenever I want, I can haul whatever, it can handle itself in the deepest mud, go up whatever old logging road, I can fish, hike, wherever. It's state-of-the-art. It's won every award this year.

ANA: It must be nice. To have your own place.

NUNO: It is.

ANA: Where are you going next?

NUNO: Nowhere special. Vancouver. I'm saving up for Hawai'i.

ANA: Are you ever worried –

NUNO: What?

ANA: The work will dry up?

NUNO: Nah. My mom's too connected. And I could always hit the road.

ANA: Go from camp to camp?

NUNO: Sure. Whatever.

ANA: I wish I was a guy.

NUNO: Why?

ANA: I could make money like you.

NUNO: Girls can get their ticket.

ANA: What? Be an insulator?

NUNO: Why not?

ANA: It's, like, 95 percent guys in your industry.

NUNO: You work with those same guys right now. And in a bar.

ANA: True. I'll think about it, getting my ticket. Hmm. Ha, I could hire an escort.

NUNO: Girls can hire escorts.

ANA: Dude, everyone watches everything I do. As far as sex goes –

NUNO: Yeah?

ANA: I'm damned if I do, damned if I don't. I'm either the town prude or the town whore.

JIMMY enters.

JIMMY: Ana.

ANA is instantly attracted to him and becomes arch, awkward, trying to compensate with speedy repartees. JIMMY is flattered. NUNO thinks only of his truck.

ANA: Jimmy.

NUNO: Jimmy.

JIMMY: Nice truck.

NUNO: Thanks, man. Yours is nice, too.

JIMMY: Thanks, man. I should think about upgrading. You happy?

NUNO: So happy.

JIMMY: Cool.

NUNO: That truck can do anything.

ANA: It's won every award this year.

JIMMY: It's amazing. What kind of beach is this?

ANA: It used to be cool, when we were kids.

JIMMY: What's up with those warning signs? Look Out. Own Risk. Surveillance cameras.

NUNO: It's owned by the smelter.

JIMMY: It's kind of creepy. Why don't you go somewhere else?

ANA: We don't have access to the water.

JIMMY: What?

NUNO: We don't have access to a beach. No one does.

JIMMY: No one in Kitimat has access to a beach?

ANA: No.

NUNO: All owned by the smelter. Or it belongs to the x̱á'isla.

JIMMY: Who?

NUNO: The First Nations people. Across the water. Over there. You know, the ones who have been here, like, nine thousand years. Or since the beginning of time. Take your pick.

JIMMY: In Rupert, I met this (*pronouncing with some difficulty*) Ts'msyen guy who was from a village that was, like, ten thousand years old.

ANA: So trippy. That's so long.

JIMMY: He says his people lost their right to fish, and now they have to eat at the soup kitchen at the Salvation Army.

ANA: That's so depressing. Look what we've done by coming here.

JIMMY: What, are you an environmentalist or something?

ANA: (*laughing awkwardly*) No, oh, god no.

NUNO: This used to be a family beach. Now they're worried about liability. Or us spying. But it's us they're spying on.

ANA: Surveillance cameras.

JIMMY: Fortunately, I look really good on camera.

NUNO: I'm going to go get more beer. (*to ANA, suddenly aware of her dynamic with JIMMY and becoming protective*) Be careful.

> *NUNO exits.*

JIMMY: (*to ANA*) You look so intellectual in those glasses.

ANA: I do like to read a book now and then.

JIMMY: I do like coming to the Ol' Keg now and then.

ANA: Shut up.

JIMMY: I do!

ANA: Can't get enough of a bar with fluorescent lights?

JIMMY: Temporary workers, eating as many wings as they can …

ANA: Pounding back the pitchers of beer.

JIMMY: Before their bus leaves at 10 p.m.

ANA: Back to work camp.

JIMMY: To me, it's heaven.

ANA: Shut up.

JIMMY: Because it's where I can see you, looking so officious. Ordering everyone around.

ANA: It's my job. I'm the shift supervisor.

JIMMY: I love women in power.

ANA: It's not much power.

JIMMY: Could've fooled me. What do your eyes look like behind those things?

>*ANA takes her glasses off.*

JIMMY: Beautiful.

ANA: Shut up.

JIMMY: Okay.

>*JIMMY kisses her. ANA kisses back. NUNO comes back.*

NUNO: I thought I said be careful!

JIMMY: I thought you were going to get beer.

NUNO: It was in the car.

>*ANA is embarrassed and looks down.*

NUNO: Dude, you better not hurt my cousin.

ANA: Nuno!

NUNO: What?

ANA: I can handle myself.

ACT ONE – Scene Nine

>*The Viveiros bedroom, January 2014. JULIA pulls a statue of Mary out from a drawer and places it on the nightstand. She kneels and prays. CLARA and JOSÉ enter and watch her. Then MANNY enters the bedroom and is startled to see JULIA on her knees.*

MANNY: You're praying?

> *JULIA rises and stuffs Mary back in the drawer.*

JULIA: I can't. I'm still too angry.

MANNY: Oh querida.

> *MANNY holds JULIA, who starts to cry. CLARA and JOSÉ approach JULIA, kiss her. JULIA feels this like a soft, comforting, quiet wind. Then CLARA and JOSÉ exit.*

JULIA: I miss them.

MANNY: Me too.

JULIA: That pipeline. How can we know it's safe?

MANNY: We don't.

JULIA: Why does Marta say it will be the safest one ever built?

MANNY: I don't know. Maybe she believes it.

JULIA: When I close my eyes, I see Barb and me out in the kayak last summer, the sea and the sky mixing in a silvery blue. Yellow sea grasses, red berries, green cedars, bottle-brown seaweed drifting in the water – and then, (*starting to cry*) a leak, oil, bitumen, billowing, sinking, becoming a great mass. I can't stop it. Seabirds, seals, otters, all choking in it. That's what we're risking. And my sister, she's behind this. She's part of making that pipeline come here. Manny –

MANNY: It could happen.

JULIA: That's supposed to make me feel better?

MANNY: Would you rather I should lie?

JULIA: How are you going to vote? In the plebiscite?

MANNY: I'm going to vote yes. Aren't you?

JULIA: I'm not sure.

MANNY: We need the jobs. Querida, we came here for work. That's why we live here.

JULIA: How did it get this way? We used to live off the land and the sea. Not corporations.

MANNY: I don't know, meu amor.

ACT ONE – Scene Ten

Kitimat, 1958. The CHORUS enters: CHORISTER 1 as a journalist and the rest of the CHORISTERS as planners and residents of Kitimat. Flash of a camera. CHORISTER 1 is taking a picture of other CHORISTERS and interviewing them as part of the publicity for the new town.

CHORISTER 4: We admire Americans. For the way they dig up mountains, change the course of rivers.

CHORISTER 2: For how they throw the map all over the place.

CHORISTER 4: And that's just what Canadians are doing in Kitimat.

CHORISTER 5: All that mud everywhere is a memory.

CHORISTER 4: We built a hell of a dam. Made an inland sea. As large as Connecticut. Plus half of Rhode Island.

CHORISTER 1 composes CHORISTERS 4 and 5 in a macho pose and takes another picture.

CHORISTER 5: Now water plummets through generators. Singing with more kilowatts than any other hydroelectric plant in the world today.

CHORISTER 1 composes CHORISTERS 2 and 3 in a pose suggesting a 1950s vision of the future (arms akimbo, faces turned upwards and showing off determined jawlines, ready for anything ...) and takes another picture.

CHORISTER 3: At the smelter, a tap, no, a touch, no, a whisper of electricity transforms bauxite ore into aluminum, the miracle metal.

CHORISTER 2: In the carefully planned frontier metropolis.

CHORISTER 1 composes CHORISTERS 2 and 6 in a 1950s "domestic" pose (classic nuclear family, with the wife doing housework ecstatically, or similar) and takes another picture.

CHORISTER 6: Kitimat is a good place to raise children.

CHORISTER 2: The "garden city" plan. Walkways separate cars from pedestrians.

CHORISTER 6: You can raise 'em up. Without fear of someone striking 'em down.

CHORISTER 2: Everyone has pride.

CHORISTER 6: In making, building, creating ...

CHORISTER 1: Kitimat.

ACT ONE – Scene Eleven

BARB's place, January 2014.

JULIA: I feel so stupid. Ashamed.

BARB: Why?

JULIA: It's taking me so long to understand.

BARB: You're not the only one feeling intimidated.

JULIA: Is everyone in Kitimat supposed to read this *National Energy Board Report*, all the legal testimony, to be able to vote?

BARB: It's an old lawyer's tactic. Bury 'em under paperwork.

JULIA: And Marta, all these reassuring phrases she's using – "safest pipeline ever built," "world-class cleanup" – compared to what? How does anybody get the courage to stand up to these pipeline people?

BARB: You need some inspiration?

JULIA: I do.

BARB pulls out a laptop and makes a few clicks.

BARB: These are people like us. Who are speaking out. (*pointing to the screen*) Nancy Nyce. She's x̄á'isla. From Kitamaat Village. You know the one, only ten kilometres away.

JULIA: (*sarcastically*) I've heard of it ... (*laughing*) since I was born. I don't know why our city planners couldn't have given our municipality a completely different name, rather than taking over theirs, give or take one or two vowels.

BARB: I know, right? Nancy Nyce was asked to speak when this group of famous women, one of whom was a Nobel Prize winner, came to Kitimat.

JULIA: Wait – the Nobel Prize?

BARB: Yup.

JULIA: That's huge.

BARB: I know.

JULIA: And they came here?

BARB: Yes.

> BARB *plays a video on her laptop.* CHORUS *members enter as participants in the videos* BARB *and* JULIA *are watching.*

CHORISTER 1: (*as x̄á'isla activist and advisor Nancy Nyce*) It's not just for the x̄á'isla and First Nations people or one specific ethnic group. It's time for everyone to stand up and be heard. As mothers and grandmothers, it's about the health of your children. It's about each and every one of you and your physical health. You don't know what toxins they're going to be allowing you to eat.

BARB: This one is –

JULIA: I know him!

BARB: Right. He's in our group. This is him testifying to the National Energy Board.

CHORISTER 2: We appeal to the world. We are a gem under siege.

BARB: This one is from Kalamazoo, Michigan. In 2010, they had the largest inland oil spill in history.

JULIA: People from Kalamazoo came here?

> BARB *nods.*

CHORISTER 3: After the oil spill, my husband has been having seizures every day. He'll never be the same.

JULIA: Who are we, who is Marta, to ignore these people?

BARB: Here's another one from Kalamazoo.

CHORISTER 4: See, they put some sand on top of it in the river and called it a cleanup. But all you have to do is kick it, and the oil is right there.

JULIA: That one. Exxon Valdez spill. They came here too?

> BARB *nods.*

CHORISTER 5: Our town is ruined.

CHORISTER 6: Don't let them ruin yours.

> JULIA *covers her mouth. Her eyes fill with tears.*

ACT ONE – Scene Twelve

Outside the Ol' Keg Pub, January 2014. NUNO and ANA are shivering.

ANA: I can handle myself.

NUNO: Really?

ANA: I like him. Can't I hang out with him?

NUNO: Some of these guys are such sweet talkers.

ANA: He's not. He is the opposite.

NUNO: Ana, you could have your pick of guys.

ANA: They're all temporary workers, Nuno. And a few guys from high school who got hired on to make big money. What the hell am I supposed to do?

NUNO: Wait. Go get your ticket in a trade. Or go to college. Date guys then.

ANA: I've missed all the applications. I'm stuck here, like, another year or two. Think of Jimmy as my free escort.

NUNO: Seriously?

ANA: Seriously. I don't want to wait, like, two more years. For love or whatever. I'm too nervous. I feel like such an idiot. Being so inexperienced. If I slept with someone from town, everyone would know. They'd be all psycho into marrying me or whatever.

NUNO: I thought you wanted to get married.

ANA: Not to anyone around here.

NUNO: Okay, but be careful.

ANA: Thanks. Town sure looks ridiculous. "Yes for Kitimat" signs everywhere. That must cost a ton of money.

NUNO: The oil company is freaking out.

ANA: Why do they care?

NUNO: Every town in the north is against it but us. If we vote yes, it'll prove it should happen.

ACT ONE – Scene Thirteen

The da Terra bedroom, 1958. Music cue. CLARA enters, unpacks a statue of Mary from a drawer, and prays to her.

CLARA: Nossa Senhora.[16]

JOSÉ enters and watches her.

JOSÉ: Clara, I am sorry to disturb.

CLARA: How are you?

JOSÉ: Today was hard.

JOSÉ collapses on the bed. CLARA tries to reach out to him, but stops herself. JOSÉ studies her face, then says longingly:

JOSÉ: Would you tell me a story? Some story of home?

CLARA: I do not know what –

JOSÉ: Anything.

CLARA: You have saudade for home. The great longing.

JOSÉ: For what can never be.

CLARA moves over. JOSÉ sits, gingerly, on the bed. As he listens, he becomes comforted by her words.

CLARA: A long time ago, Queen Isabel saw that her people were starving, so she brought them bread. When her husband, the king, discovered Isabel doing this, he was furious. He forbid Isabel to ever give bread to her people again.

JOSÉ: Why would he do that?

CLARA: Maybe he thought it made him look bad, who knows.

JOSÉ: He forbid it?

CLARA: Yes, but Queen Isabel knew in her heart that this was not right. So she hid bread in her cloak and snuck out, whenever she could, to feed the people. Then one day, one terrible day, the shortest day of the year, the coldest of cold winter days, the king caught Isabel going out.

JOSÉ: Oh no.

---

16 Our Lady.

CLARA: He said, "Queen Isabel!" She said, "Yes, my lord?" He said, "What are you hiding there?"

> *JULIA enters and watches CLARA and JOSÉ.*
> *They do not see her.*

CLARA: Now Queen Isabel did not know what to answer. For she knew the king could lock her away, forever, maybe even burn her at the stake.

JOSÉ: Oh no.

CLARA: So Queen Isabel decided to tell a lie. A lie to save her life. She said, "My lord, it is only roses." Then the king laughed. For he knew he had trapped her. It was the dead of winter and no one had seen a rose for months and months. He said, "My Queen, I demand that you open your cloak!" Isabel was terrified and began to tremble.

JOSÉ: She didn't want to die.

CLARA: She did not.

JOSÉ: So what did she do?

CLARA: She opened her cloak and roses fell out.

JOSÉ: (*smiling*) Oh.

> *The CHORUS enters as folk musicians and dancers. They*
> *dance the chamarrita and hand out roses. JULIA exits.*

CLARA: The Espírito Santo, the Holy Spirit, protected her. Just like the Espírito Santo protects those who feed the hungry, those who do right, even when it seems impossible.

> *JOSÉ hands CLARA money. She is overcome by his generosity.*
> *She knows this will change the lives of those back in their*
> *village of Achadinha, in the Azores.*

JOSÉ: Clara, meu amor, would you mail this home? To your friends and family who go hungry. In honour of Queen Isabel.

CLARA: Oh, José, querido. Muito obrigada.[17]

JOSÉ: De nada.[18]

---

17 Oh, José, dear. Thank you.
18 You're welcome.

ACT ONE – Scene Fourteen

*The Viveiros home, January 2014. JULIA and MARTA are
going through their parents' belongings. MARTA is efficiently
opening a cardboard box and sorting through it. JULIA tries
to open Clara's suitcase but is overcome.*

JULIA: I can't.

MARTA: Maybe what's inside will bring happy memories.

JULIA: Those are the ones that hurt the most.

MARTA: Oh, Julia.

JULIA still can't open the suitcase.

MARTA: Let me.

MARTA opens the suitcase.

MARTA: Mom's sunglasses. (*putting them on*) Do I look like Amália?

JULIA: The Queen of Fado. Yes.

MARTA: She made being Portuguese cool. (*finding some clip-on earrings*)
These are so '50s. Do you remember how she would tease up her hair?

JULIA: Her hair was so high, she could have hid a loaf of bread in there.

MARTA and JULIA laugh.

MARTA: Oh my god. The Sears catalogue.

JULIA: What's that doing in there?

MARTA: She and her friends learned English from it. Remember how
she'd say "brassiere"?

JULIA: Yes. I hated when she took me downtown to be fitted for a
"brassiere."

*MARTA and JULIA laugh. JULIA pulls a 1960s woman's suit
out of the box. She breathes in the smell, then begins to cry.*

JULIA: (*handing MARTA the suit*) Mom's suit. Here, you take it.

MARTA: Are you sure?

JULIA: You're the businesswoman.

JULIA pulls some heels out of the box, slips them on, and walks in them.

MARTA: You look like a movie star.

JULIA: (*sadly*) That's what Dad used to say.

MARTA: Keep them.

JULIA: Thanks, Marta. They're so like Mom.

JULIA can't do any more. She starts to sit and cry. MARTA comforts her.

MARTA: Why don't you come to church?

JULIA: I'm –

MARTA: Are you angry? At God? I was.

JULIA: I am. They suffered so much.

MARTA: I know, but we draw our strength from our community. From our faith.

JULIA: It was wrong.

MARTA: I know. They didn't have the science back then to protect them.

JULIA: Do they have the science to protect us now?

MARTA: Julia, it's an emotional day. Let's not talk about this now.

JULIA: Why did you call for this plebiscite?

MARTA: City Council serves the people. We should know what they think.

JULIA: Are you giving the oil company a free public-opinion poll?

JULIA dumps out one box, then starts quickly loading things into it: old magazines and papers to be recycled, etc.

JULIA: Is it true? Kitimat has its first homeless people?

JULIA unfurls a garbage bag and puts the heels into it, along with some clothing.

MARTA: Julia, you're upset.

JULIA: You bet I am. Our first homeless people? Ever?

MARTA: It's of great concern to City Council. There are bumps along the road.

JULIA: People shouldn't be bumps along the road.

> *JULIA begins chucking things into the garbage bags, faster and faster.*

MARTA: Could you slow down?

JULIA: It's time for it to go. I read the testimony to the National Energy Board. I can't get it out of my head. Chief Ellis Ross spoke about how we've killed off the x̄á'isla's food stocks, the abalone, the oolichan fish.

MARTA: We didn't personally do that.

JULIA: No, but the industry here did. From their perspective, we came in here, sixty years ago, and poisoned the place. Why can't the x̄á'isla vote in this plebiscite?

MARTA: They live in their own village, where they have their own votes.

JULIA: Yes, and they're against this pipeline.

MARTA: The federal government is making all sorts of deals with them. It's not like they're against all the proposed projects coming in.

JULIA: What are they supposed to do to live? Now that their fish are gone?

MARTA: What are we supposed to do? To live?

JULIA: I don't know. Move on.

MARTA: To where? Kitimat is all we know. Julia, I know it's not easy – me being in politics. I really appreciate you being supportive. It means so much. It's essential. Thank you for your faith in me. We're going to do well by this, Julia, I promise.

ACT ONE – Scene Fifteen

A hotel room at the Kitimat Lodge, January 2014.

ANA: Jimmy, it was really sweet of you to get this hotel room.

JIMMY: I'm a sweet guy.

ANA: This place is nice.

JIMMY: You seem surprised.

ANA: It's kinda cool. Like a mountain lodge. I love the trees. I feel like a Sasquatch could come out of the woods. See? It looks like his eyes are way back there in the trees, looking at us, seeing what we're going to do.

JIMMY: Do you think he's watching us?

ANA: My grandma used to say God watches everything we do. And if we confess all our sins, we can make everything right in the world.

JIMMY: Um, forgive me, Ana, but, all this talk of Sasquatch and God, it's kind of a turnoff.

ANA: Ever wonder? What it would be like to sleep all night together, and wake up together, and –

JIMMY: Stop right there. Let's not take this so seriously.

ANA is looking the other way. JIMMY takes his shirt off and crosses towards her.

ANA: What do you want to talk about?

JIMMY: I don't really want to talk at all.

ANA turns and is stunned by the fact JIMMY's half naked and so close. They kiss. JIMMY pulls out a condom. They make their way to the bed. ANA is so passionate she accidentally knocks him down. JIMMY senses something is a bit off.

JIMMY: Let's slow down. Let's relax.

ANA crosses to the beers and begins downing one as fast as she can. JIMMY gets a beer too.

ANA: They used to call this place the Paradise.

JIMMY: That's a good name for it. The Paradise.

ANA: Then they called it the Parasite.

JIMMY: (*laughing, spitting out some beer*) You're so funny.

ANA: What? They do. Call it the Parasite. But they seem to be fixing it up.

JIMMY: Hence all the construction paper all over the front.

ANA: Hence?

JIMMY: I like to read a book now and then, too.

ANA: Do you know the nickname for the Kitimat Hotel?

JIMMY: Yup. The Zoo. Have you been there?

ANA shakes her head.

ANA: Some call it the centre of sin.

JIMMY: It's pretty rough. The waitress wears a ferret. I mean, she wears clothes, too … I mean, there are strippers there, but the waitress – Why am I nervous? I must really like you. Let's just say they call it the Zoo for a reason.

> *ANA kisses JIMMY. It gets more passionate. She tries to unbuckle his belt. It's not going well.*

JIMMY: Wait – Have you ever done this before?

ANA: No.

JIMMY: Wow. You act so –

ANA: So what? Slutty?

JIMMY: Into it. Jeez. Ana. I don't know. It's your first time?

ANA: So what?

JIMMY: That's unusual. Nothing in high school?

ANA: This is a small town.

JIMMY: What's that got to do with it?

ANA: Some of us can't stand rumours.

JIMMY: Whoa.

ANA: What's wrong?

JIMMY: I'm not sure if I'm up for being that significant.

ANA: At what?

JIMMY: In your life.

ANA: Don't worry. You won't be.

JIMMY: Thanks a lot.

ANA: I can't sleep with anybody around here. Everyone will know by the next day. I'll be half married or the town slut. Please. I want to do it. It doesn't have to be that big a deal.

JIMMY: You're sure?

ANA: I'm sure.

> *They kiss. This time, it's very sweet and sensual.*

ACT ONE – Scene Sixteen

The da Terra living room, 1958. Music fades in and out.

CLARA: (*handing JOSÉ his denim work pants*) I cannot get the dark stuff out.

JOSÉ: Don't wash in the machine.

CLARA: I didn't.

JOSÉ: The machine is so nice. We don't want to ruin it. I hear that stuff can ruin the machine.

CLARA: You told me. I wash in the sink in the garage. But it is impossible to get out.

CLARA bursts into tears.

JOSÉ: It's okay, Clara.

CLARA: Our village, in the Azores. So tiny. So warm. It is so big here. Cold.

JOSÉ gives CLARA an awkward hug, then releases her. She notices his skin.

CLARA: You burn. In the sun. It is very strange. We never burn. We have Portuguese skin.

JOSÉ: The chemicals. It is a chemical burn. They give us a cream, but it doesn't work.

CLARA: Tell me.

JOSÉ: Is not for a lady to hear.

CLARA: Tell me.

JOSÉ: Most of the men quit on the first day. The smoke. The fumes.

CLARA: Please tell me, José. I won't tell anyone back home.

JOSÉ: Promise?

CLARA: They have such hopes for us. I know.

JOSÉ: Marrying a man who is so disgusting at the end of the day.

CLARA: Oh, José. I am the one who lets you down.

JOSÉ: How?

CLARA: I cannot order the right food at the grocery. I do not know when English classes start. I cannot get the stains out of your clothes. I am still ... without ... child. What kind of wife – I disappoint –

JOSÉ: No, Clara. You don't. First of all, no one can clean these coveralls. It's pitch mixed with soot. Your cooking is wonderful. And being without a child – yet – gives us more time to practise.

CLARA: Tell me more of your work. Don't you trust me?

JOSÉ: There was an explosion. They call it a "defense." This paste leaks into the bath, which is nine hundred degrees, and then explodes: flames and black smoke is all you see. I ran and ran. But I thought none of us was going to live.

CLARA thinks of how scary it would be if she lost JOSÉ.

JOSÉ: Clara, would you – oh, never mind.

CLARA: What?

JOSÉ: Sing me a song from back home.

CLARA: I need the village. We all sing together.

JOSÉ: I know.

CLARA: The song my father used to sing with me was all about "Don't get married, we can't afford the dowry." But I heard this Portuguese song on the radio ...

JULIA enters and watches them. They do not see her.

CLARA: I bought the record. I've learned it.

CLARA sings the first verse of one of Amália Rodrigues's signature fados, "Coimbra": "Coimbra é uma lição ..."[19] As CLARA sings, JOSÉ gradually becomes more comfortable with her, and she encourages him to put his head in her lap. She strokes his hair.

---

19 Composed in 1947 by Raul Ferrão (music) and José Galhardo (lyrics). Also known in English as "April in Portugal" and "The Whisp'ring Serenade." – Playwright's note: Another Azorean folk song that could be used in this scene is "Sapateia," about a young woman falling in love with a shoemaker: "... Não há coisa que mais brilhe / Ai, que a filha dum lavradore!" (... There's nothing that could shine brighter / Ah, than a labourer's daughter!). See, on YouTube, contrasting interpretations by António Mourão (youtu.be/RohUI6XXN3Y) and the Grupo Folclórico de São Miguel (youtu.be/VxOD3uLXnr0).

*The CHORUS as Azorean villagers enter and sing after
CLARA the English lyrics to the first verse of "Coimbra."*

CHORISTER 1: (*singing*) Coimbra is a lesson ...

CHORISTER 2: (*singing*) Of dreams and traditions.

CHORISTER 3: (*singing*) The teacher is a song ...

CHORISTER 4: (*singing*) And the moon is the school.

CHORISTER 5: (*singing*) The book is a woman.

CHORISTER 6: (*singing*) Only those who learn pass
And learn to say "saudade."

ACT ONE – Scene Seventeen

*Kitimat, 1958. The CHORUS members become moviemakers
making newsreels to "sell" Kitimat to potential investors and
prospective newcomers.*

CHORISTER 1 (DIRECTOR): (*pointing to CHORISTERS 2, 4, 5, and
6, respectively*) Bea, stand there. Great, great, Fred. Joe, Ruby, right
there. Action!

*CHORISTER 3 begins rolling a film camera. CHORISTERS 2,
4, 5, and 6 act the next few lines.*

CHORISTER 2 (BEA): Brought in workers from over fifty countries.

CHORISTER 6 (RUBY): But it was up to the people to make it a town.

CHORISTER 2 (BEA): And you never know what's going to happen with
all that foreign element.

CHORISTER 4 (FRED): Kitimat became 40 percent Portuguese. Those
guys were hard workers.

CHORISTER 6 (RUBY): The government brought 'em in cuz they had
"hardened hands."

CHORISTER 2 (BEA): But they sure as heck couldn't speak English.

CHORISTER 4 (FRED): Hey, Joe, could you bring me a wrench?

CHORISTER 5 (JOE): O quê?

CHORISTER 4 (FRED): O quê?

CHORISTER 5 (JOE): O quê?

CHORISTER 4 (FRED): He says, "O quê" ... Now that really slows down a job.

CHORISTER 5 (JOE): Ah, uma chave!

CHORISTER 5 (JOE) hands CHORISTER 4 (FRED) a wrench.

CHORISTER 6 (RUBY): I guess "chave" is Portuguese for wrench.

CHORISTER 2 (BEA): Sometimes I'm at the bus stop, and I hear so much Portuguese, I think, "What? Am I living in Portugal?"

CHORISTER 1 (DIRECTOR): CUT! That's great, everybody, just great. Going to show everyone how fun it is to live here. We'll cut in some nice whimsical music. Bosses are going to love it.

CHORISTER 4 (FRED): Why do we have so many foreign workers?

CHORISTER 1 (DIRECTOR): No one expected it, but Canada has high employment. So we've got to take the ones who don't speak English. Make it seem fun.

CHORISTER 4 (FRED): Gotcha.

CHORISTER 5 (JOE) watches, sizing them up.

ACT ONE – Scene Eighteen

The Viveiros living room, January 2014.

MANNY: What do you want me to say?

JULIA: That I can speak up.

MANNY: How?

JULIA: In any way I can.

MANNY: Against Marta?

JULIA: I'm afraid so.

MANNY: In public?

JULIA: Yes.

MANNY: Wow.

JULIA: Do you really think you could lose your job?

MANNY: I've seen it happen before. When people object to industry and what it does.

The CHORUS enters as ghosts of former Kitimat residents and stands in a group.

JULIA: Why do we have to risk so much?

MANNY: It's better than it was back in Portugal.

JULIA: Is it?

MANNY: You never grew up under fascism.

JULIA: No, I didn't.

MANNY: (*pause*) Julia, making money is what I came here to do.

JULIA: Do you think we could make it with what we've saved?

MANNY: I guess.

JULIA: Manny, I know you feel like I do.

MANNY: I do.

JULIA: Aren't you tired of keeping quiet?

MANNY: (*pause*) Silence. It's what we had to do. To be safe.

*The CHORUS begins whispering the words
"Speak out, speak up ..."*

JULIA: I know. But –

MANNY: You don't think less of me, do you?

JULIA: Why would I ever do that?

MANNY: For keeping my mouth shut.

JULIA: No. I understand.

MANNY: Let's say you speak out. Are you prepared for all of the consequences? The unforeseen ones – like having to leave, hurting Ana, Nuno –

JULIA: (*pause*) There's no way I can be prepared for all of them. Scientists say if we burn the fuel in the Alberta tar sands, it's game over for us. Precisely when we should be slowing down, switching to other forms of fuel, we're speeding up, going faster and faster. Crazy ambitious.

MANNY: Julia, all of Kitimat was built with that kind of ambition.

Enter the CLARA and JOSÉ as ghosts.

JULIA: I know. Do you remember what Dad used to say about people racking up profit?

MANNY: Yup. He'd say …

MANNY & JOSÉ: "The only land any of us inherit is our grave."

JULIA: And Mom used to talk about …

JULIA & CLARA: Queen Isabel. And charity.

MANNY: You can't give charity if you have no money.

JULIA: But we're not here for long. What about what we leave for the next generations?

The CHORUS becomes more audible: "Speak out, speak up …"

MANNY: (*pause*) Do it. Speak up.

JULIA: Are you sure?

MANNY: Yes. Speak out.

JULIA considers, crosses to the front of the stage, looks straight at the audience, and decides.

JULIA: I will.

ACT TWO – Scene One

The meeting room of Kitimat's City Hall, January 2014. JULIA is speaking to City Council. MARTA is sitting nearby, smiling, as if everything is fine. (As in act one, scene five, this is possibly staged among the audience.)

MANNY is watching on TV at home. The CHORUS enters as residents of Kitimat, also watching the City Council meeting on TV.

JULIA: Greetings, Mayor and Council.

MARTA: I remind you that you have two time periods to speak, of two minutes each.

JULIA: Thank you. I object to the wording of the plebiscite. It's too complicated.

MARTA: Council has already voted on the wording of the plebiscite. It's been approved.

JULIA: Vote on it again.

MANNY: (*at home*) That's my Julia.

JULIA: The wording is too complicated. It sounds like you are trying to keep people from voting. Especially seniors and the many people in Kitimat who have English as their second language.

MANNY: (*waving a paper with the plebiscite question on it*) Ask her what the hell this is supposed to mean.

JULIA: What does this mean? People are supposed to vote on this? (*reading*) "Do you support the final report recommendations of the Joint Review Panel (JRP) of the Canadian Environmental Assessment Agency and National Energy Board, that the pipeline project presently under consideration be approved, subject to 209 conditions set out in volume two of the JRP's final report?" – What does this plebiscite ask us? If we approve of the *National Energy Board Report*? Or the pipeline? And what if we object to one of the 209 conditions?

MANNY cheers.

MARTA: I think you underestimate the people of Kitimat.

JULIA: I do not.

MARTA: Your first time slot is up.

MANNY: You can do it, querida!

JULIA: Why is this plebiscite non-binding?

MARTA: What do you want? For us to sue the national government?

MANNY exhales – he doesn't know.

JULIA: I'm not sure. If they put the pipeline in, against our will, maybe we should.

MARTA: Thank you for your presentation.

JULIA: Thank you for your attention.

JULIA exits, puts on her coat, hat, boots, and goes outside, back to her home. MARTA, an accomplished politician, is still smiling, but she exits in the opposite direction.

ACT TWO – Scene Two

January 2014. The CHORUS members transform into oil-industry executives.

CHORISTER 1: Our challenge …

CHORISTER 2: Energy security.

CHORISTER 3: Independence.

CHORISTER 4: Freedom.

CHORISTER 5: Protecting our Way of Life.

CHORISTER 6: Our solution …

CHORISTER 1: A 1,117-kilometre pipeline.

CHORISTER 2: From the Alberta oil sands to Kitimat, British Columbia.

CHORISTER 3: We'll make the transfer from land to marine environments.

CHORISTER 4: Ship export oil to Asia.

CHORISTER 5: The challenge …

CHORISTER 6: To be responsible to our shareholders.

CHORISTER 1: And those who use our products.

ALL: Oil.

CHORISTER 2: It's our most valuable resource.

CHORISTER 6: It's our solution.

ALL smile.

ACT TWO – Scene Three

The Viveiros home, January 2014. MARTA and JULIA are meeting. They stare at each other, angry and uncertain what to say. MARTA looks away.

MARTA: You had real gumption. Standing up to me like that. In front of everybody.

JULIA: Thanks.

MARTA: You were clear, you were on point, if it were any other circumstance, I'd be proud.

JULIA: Thank you.

MARTA: But what has your little exercise in democracy gotten us?

JULIA: (*silence*) I don't know. My points were good.

MARTA: All you did, Julia, was reduce people's faith. In me. Their trust. And that's something that's taken me years to build. How long have you known those nature people?

JULIA: Barb was Mom's nurse –

MARTA: I know, but how long have you been hanging out with them, discussing these things? A few weeks? I'm afraid for you, Julia. How do you know they have your best interests at heart? Why can't they stand up to me in City Council, and not you? They're turning you into a weapon. Against me.

JULIA: You're being so emotional.

MARTA: How can I not be? You just humiliated me in front of all of Kitimat. Julia, we need to stick together.

JULIA: What do you mean by "stick together"? What do you want me to do? Keep quiet?

MARTA: That would be a good start.

JULIA: I can't.

MARTA: Why not?

JULIA: All those people – from real and terrible oil spills. They came to warn us.

MARTA: Those people are backed by interests outside of Canada. Hollywood celebrities. Environmentalists.

JULIA: What's wrong with that?

MARTA: How do you know they have our best interests at heart? (*noticing a map of Canada on the wall*) Julia, you put the map back up. Why?

JULIA: I'm trying to teach myself.

MARTA: About what? (*referring to the map*) What's all that writing?

JULIA: Where all the spills were, where the pipeline is supposed to go, how it's all connected.

MARTA: I'm impressed.

JULIA: That's kind of patronizing. But thanks.

MARTA: It must be something you feel very strongly about, to risk our family in this way.

JULIA: I do.

MARTA: But Julia, you've been studying this for a few weeks, I've been living and working in it for years –

JULIA: How do you know what's best?

MARTA: I do. I do know what's best. For our family.

JULIA: Our family. Are you talking about how you took care of Dad?

MARTA: You know damn well I was in university then. He didn't want me to drop out. You and Manny – I didn't mean for it to happen, but I can see how you'd feel that you were railroaded into taking care of them.

JULIA: I don't.

MARTA: I could see why you'd resent me.

JULIA: This isn't about that.

MARTA: Are you sure?

JULIA: Fine. Maybe I did want to go to university.

MARTA: What's wrong?

JULIA: You know, I find it so sad that Mom, no matter how sick she was, when you were coming over, she'd make me help her get dressed up. She'd be throwing up or … god, I don't even want to say. She was so thin, and she'd make me put on her full makeup, her best clothes. Even if it hurt her. I'd say, "It's just Marta, Mom," and she'd say, "Don't talk that way about your sister. She's a somebody."

MARTA: They were proud of you, too.

JULIA: Not like that. You're the first woman in our family to go to university. But other people can think, you know.

MARTA: I'm not saying you can't.

JULIA: Aren't you?

MARTA: Julia, do you know what Dad asked me to do before he died?

JULIA: No.

MARTA: He asked me to look out for the family. Our finances. And haven't I always done that?

JULIA: Yes.

MARTA: Looked out for you? And Manny and Nuno and Ana? Haven't I been generous?

JULIA: You have.

MARTA: Even if you and your new friends do manage to organize against this pipeline, and, say, sure, we vote against it, the federal government will override us. They'll put it in anyways.

JULIA: Then what's the point?

MARTA: Exactly. Ever since I called for a plebiscite, I've been seeing people fight. They're losing friends and family over this. I don't want that to be us. Do you?

JULIA: No.

MARTA: (*embracing JULIA*) I love you. Don't let them mess with that.

JULIA looks very stressed, but keeps silent and nods.

JULIA: I won't.

ACT TWO – Scene Four

Outside the Ol' Keg Pub, February 2014.

ANA: She took my hand and she said that, for her, Kitimat was a kind of heaven. She told me Kitimat was strange in those days. Everyone in their twenties like us. She told me there was no grey hair and no death – except now and then from an accident. More babies here than any other postal code in Canada. And no grandparents to show them to.

NUNO: That's so weird. Our moms had no grandparents.

ANA: I know.

NUNO: I hope you don't think Kitimat can be like that again.

ANA: Like what?

NUNO: A place to fall in love, raise a family. It's not like that now.

ANA: I know.

NUNO: Jimmy's not like that.

ANA: I know.

NUNO: I think he's got a lady in every town. Kids even.

ANA: Really?

NUNO: Surprised?

ANA: He's not that smooth.

NUNO: I'm looking out for you, coz. I'll beat him up –

ANA: Nuno, seriously?

NUNO: If he hurts you.

ANA: I can look out for myself.

NUNO: You always say that, but I'm not so sure.

ANA: I can. Nuno, how did it get like this? Everybody in Kitimat is afraid to talk. They're keeping their mouths shut about the plebiscite. Do you think they're fighting at home? Like our moms?

NUNO: Your mom has always been emotional, but –

ANA: What do you mean, "emotional"?

NUNO: Ana, she's tripping out about whales. She's hanging out with birdwatchers. She's becoming a hippy nerd.

ANA: What about *your* mom? She's so ... sure of herself.

NUNO: Isn't that good? Especially for a woman.

ANA: Like she should be my role model? I'll never be a suit.

NUNO: Why not? You'd make more money.

ANA: She's obsessed with jobs. She ignores scientific evidence.

NUNO: You don't know that!

ANA: My mom's not a hippy!

NUNO: Are we fighting?

ANA: Not us too.

NUNO: I hope it's not contagious.

ANA: It feels like our family is falling apart.

NUNO: Yeah.

ACT TWO – Scene Five

The da Terra dining room, 1958. Music cue. CLARA and JOSÉ are trying to write a letter home.

JOSÉ: Their letters to us are like a fairy tale.

CLARA: What you mean?

JOSÉ: Your mother writes: "You go to make your fortune ..."

CLARA: "... in the land of ice and snow." She pays a lady in the village to write for her. She wants to be poetic. But I don't know what to write back.

JOSÉ: They pin their hopes to us.

CLARA: We are like pincushions.

JOSÉ: We should write that you are becoming very glamorous. Like a movie star.

CLARA: What? In all this mud?

JOSÉ hands her a shoebox containing a pair of elegant heels.

CLARA: Oh José!

JOSÉ: I saw you looking at them in the window. Now you can be a real Canadian lady.

CLARA puts on the shoes and walks.

CLARA: I feel like a movie star.

JOSÉ: You look like one. There is something else ... in the box.

CLARA discovers earrings and sunglasses, like something Amália Rodrigues would wear around 1958. She laughs and puts them on.

CLARA: Yes, we will write to them about our expensive tastes. For shoes and refrigerators.

JOSÉ: Do you think these tastes mean we can't go back?

CLARA: No. I would give up every shoe, every refrigerator if I could see them again. So would you. But they need us to send money back, not spend it on a trip to see them.

JOSÉ: If you could go back, right now, what would you do?

CLARA: I would buy everyone wine. One night. Be a big roller.

JOSÉ: Where did you hear that? "Big roller"?

CLARA: On the TV. It means someone who spends lots of money. A gambler.

JOSÉ: (*laughing*) Your English is getting so good!

CLARA: Obrigada.

JOSÉ: These letters. What should we write to them? Could they make their fortune too? In the land of snow?

CLARA: I don't know. Sometimes it is so hard in the smelter. And missing home, it's like a wound –

JOSÉ: That will never heal. I wouldn't want to be fighting for Salazar in Angola. Or to be thrown in prison for saying the wrong thing. It is better here. We will tell them to come.

CLARA: They can stay with us. There is so much room.

JOSÉ smiles at CLARA; he's proud of her.

ACT TWO – Scene Six

A board room, February 2014. The CHORUS members enter as oil-industry publicists. They're having a private meeting.

CHORISTER 1: The plebiscite. Any thoughts?

CHORISTER 2: It could be huge for us if we win.

CHORISTER 3: We should keep quiet. If we hit them too hard, they could get ticked off.

CHORISTER 4: That's what we all did after the spill in the Gulf. It got us nowhere.

CHORISTER 5: We've got to put a stake in the ground.

CHORISTER 6: We've got to be a part of the conversation.

CHORISTER 2: We've got to initiate the conversation.

CHORISTER 1: Change our reputation.

CHORISTER 3: Why do they get to be the local ones, the ones who care about the environment, the scientific ones?

CHORISTER 4: I've got it. We *are* all those things.

CHORISTER 3: Local?

CHORISTER 4: Yes.

CHORISTER 3: Environmental?

CHORISTER 4: Yes.

CHORISTER 3: Scientific?

CHORISTER 4: Yes.

CHORISTER 1: People, let's make some ads.

ACT TWO – Scene Seven

A call centre somewhere in Alberta, February 2014. TIM is sitting at a desk and wearing a headset microphone. He glances nervously at the text on his computer screen. He clears his throat, then dials his phone, which rings in the Viveiros home. As the scene progresses and TIM is conducting phone polls, each interviewed character is discovered in their own environment.

MANNY: (*answering his phone*) Hello?

TIM: Good evening. Am I speaking to Mr. Viva?

MANNY: Viveiros. Who are you?

TIM: Good evening, sir. Do you have a few moments to take a poll?

During the next section, as an ongoing backdrop to the following scenes, CHORUS members enter as pollsters, carrying landline phones. They begin phoning people, asking: "Do you have a few moments to take a poll? Do you drive a car? On a scale of one to five, how do you feel about the energy industry?"

MANNY: (*to TIM*) Who is this?

TIM: I work for an independent polling company.

MANNY: What's your name?

TIM: Tim.

MANNY: Tim, was your independent polling company hired by the pipeline company?

TIM: Why is that relevant, sir?

> *TIM hangs up.*
>
> *Meanwhile, JULIA, at home, reads off her computer screen.*
>
> *TIM calls MARTA, who answers on her cell.*

MARTA: Hello?

TIM: Do you have a few moments to take a poll?

MARTA: Of course.

TIM: Do you drive a vehicle?

MARTA: Yes.

TIM: On a scale of one to five, how do you feel about the energy industry?

MARTA: Five. It's what gives us a good life in Kitimat. A great life.

TIM: Thank you so much.

MARTA: You're welcome.

TIM: Not everyone is so gracious, especially about being polled on their cellphone.

MARTA: I understand. Cell polling is the best way to reach young voters.

TIM: It is.

> *TIM hangs up and calls the Viveiros residence.*

JULIA: (*picking up*) Hello?

TIM: Good evening. Am I speaking to Mrs. Viva?

JULIA: Viveiros.

TIM: Do you have a few moments to take a poll?

JULIA: Didn't you call yesterday?

TIM: I did. But I didn't speak with the lady of the house. Do you drive a vehicle?

JULIA: Yes.

TIM: On a scale of one to five, how do you feel about the energy industry?

JULIA: Of yesterday?

TIM: What?

JULIA: How I used to feel, or how I feel now?

TIM: Uh. Now. I guess.

JULIA: Do you mean the energy industry or this oil pipeline?

TIM: I'm sorry, lady. I don't write the questions.

JULIA: We need energy. Of some kind.

TIM: Yes, good. On a scale of one to five.

JULIA: Five. But you don't ask what kind of energy?

TIM: No, ma'am. I don't.

> *TIM hangs up and calls ANA.*

ANA: Hello?

TIM: Good evening. Am I speaking to Mrs. de Vivo?

ANA: Nope.

TIM: Do you have a few moments to take a poll?

ANA: Kay.

TIM: Do you drive a vehicle?

ANA: Totally. Wait, does this use up my cellphone minutes?

TIM: Yes. On a scale of one to five, how do you feel about the energy industry?

ANA: Is this about that plebiscite thing, where we vote on whether we want the pipeline?

TIM: On a scale of one to five, how would you feel –

ANA: I don't recognize your voice. Are you from Kitimat?

TIM: No.

ANA: Where are you from?

TIM: Alberta.

ANA: I find it weird that you are polling, calling people all the time, to find out what we think. Why? I thought this was just some random City Council vote thing that barely even makes sense, and now I'm starting to think that you guys, who work for the oil-pipeline company, are nervous about this vote. And that our vote actually matters. Does it?

TIM: Um. Thank you for your time.

TIM hangs up.

ACT TWO – Scene Eight

February 2014. CHORISTERS 1, 2, and 3 as, respectively, director, scientist, and cameraperson are making a commercial.

CHORISTER 1 (DIRECTOR): Action!

CHORISTER 2 (SCIENTIST): Happy Earth Day!

But CHORISTER 2 (SCIENTIST) is suddenly overcome with emotion and stops.

CHORISTER 1 (DIRECTOR): Why did you stop?

CHORISTER 2 (SCIENTIST): (*out of character*) Three hundred scientists in Canada have just signed a petition against this pipeline.

CHORISTER 1 (DIRECTOR): We know.

CHORISTER 2 (SCIENTIST): The government is dismantling science libraries, losing over a hundred years of research.

CHORISTER 1 (DIRECTOR): This isn't about that. Who funds your research?

CHORISTER 2 (SCIENTIST): The pipeline company.

CHORISTER 1 (DIRECTOR): Your research is sound, isn't it?

CHORISTER 2 (SCIENTIST): It is.

CHORISTER 1 (DIRECTOR): Focus on that. Action!

CHORISTER 2 (SCIENTIST): (*back into character*) Happy Earth Day! Here are some ways you can make a difference. Turn off the tap when you brush your teeth. Walk to work. Hug someone. These everyday actions have a huge impact on the environment.

CHORISTER 1 (DIRECTOR): Could you mention that you are a cancer survivor? That's very relatable. We're still rolling.

CHORISTER 2 (SCIENTIST): I am a cancer survivor. A nature lover. A biologist.

CHORISTER 1 (DIRECTOR): CUT! That was wonderful. Thank you so much.

ACT TWO – Scene Nine

A rock overlooking the Douglas Channel, south of Kitimat, February 2014. JULIA and MANNY enter in winter coats and contemplate the estuary.

JULIA: I love the silence of snow falling on snow.

MANNY: I love those cuts in the rocks.

JULIA: Glaciers made those as they retreated.

MANNY: It's beautiful.

MANNY kisses JULIA.

JULIA: Look at you! Mr. Outdoors.

MANNY: Look at you, Mrs. I Stood Up to My Sister in City Council.

JULIA: All this – the animals, the birds, the trees.

MANNY: They can't vote.

JULIA: No, they can't. We have to figure it out for them. You know Barb's group?

MANNY: Yes.

JULIA: The BBC called them.

MANNY: The BBC. From Britain.

JULIA: To see how we're going to vote.

MANNY: That's huge.

JULIA: I know.

MANNY: The world is watching Kitimat.

MANNY squeezes JULIA's hand; he's proud of her. They both gaze out on the incredible beauty of the place in front of them.

ACT TWO – Scene Ten

February 2014. CHORISTERS 1, 3, 4, and 5 as, respectively, director, cameraperson, project manager, and coffee-bar owner are shooting two more commercials.

CHORISTER 1 (DIRECTOR): ACTION!

CHORISTER 4 (PROJECT MANAGER): (*to the camera*) I'm the liaison for Kitimat. I live here. I love this place. I grew up here. I'm going to retire here. I'm at a time in my life when family is what matters most. Please, come see me, ask me anything. My door is always open.

CHORISTER 1 (DIRECTOR): Great. Could we see you looking out over the fields of snow? Nice. Where are your dogs?

CHORISTER 4 (PROJECT MANAGER): I don't have any dogs.

CHORISTER 1 (DIRECTOR): What? (*to CHORISTER 3 (CAMERAPERSON)*) I thought you said –

CHORISTER 3 (CAMERAPERSON): (*to CHORISTER 4 (PROJECT MANAGER)*) I thought you said –

CHORISTER 4 (PROJECT MANAGER): I'm going to get some.

CHORISTER 1 (DIRECTOR): We're going to have to reschedule.

CHORISTER 3 (CAMERAPERSON): A couple of golden retrievers would be best.

CHORISTER 5 (COFFEE-BAR OWNER) gets into place, while CHORISTER 4 (PROJECT MANAGER) exits.

CHORISTER 1 (DIRECTOR): ACTION!

CHORISTER 5 (COFFEE-BAR OWNER): (*to the camera*) My name is Adelaide da Costa. I run the coffee bar in town. It's a family business – we all have to pitch in for it to work.

CHORISTER 1 (DIRECTOR): Nice. Can you do some things around your business while you talk? Clean a counter, serve something, you know?

CHORISTER 5 (COFFEE-BAR OWNER): Of course.

CHORISTER 1 (DIRECTOR): ACTION!

CHORISTER 5 (COFFEE-BAR OWNER): (*to the camera*) I source local, sustainable ingredients whenever I can. In Kitimat, we have every kind of berry in the summer. I bake everything from scratch. My coffee bar is where the community gets together. I thought we were going to have to close, until the pipeline people started talking about coming here. Now, we can stay open. That's why I'm voting "Yes for Kitimat."

CHORISTER 1 (DIRECTOR): CUT. Terrific!

ACT TWO – Scene Eleven

Outside the Viveiros home, February 2014. TIM walks by the house. JULIA notices him and runs out to talk to him.

JULIA: What are you doing? You. Young man.

TIM: Me?

JULIA: Yes, you. What are you doing?

TIM: Talking to people. I got a promotion.

JULIA: Good for you.

TIM: Thank you, ma'am.

JULIA: What are you talking to people about? The plebiscite?

TIM: And other things.

JULIA: Why are you guys all in black? You look like a SWAT team.

TIM: I'm sure it's not intentional, ma'am.

JULIA: Why aren't you coming to our house?

TIM: We don't go to houses that are a "no" vote. It is considered a security risk.

JULIA: Me and my family are a security risk?

TIM: Yes, ma'am.

JULIA: You consider us dangerous.

TIM: We do.

JULIA: And my neighbours, do you consider them a security risk too?

TIM: Uh ... some of them.

JULIA: Do you have security guards with you?

TIM: Yes ma'am, we do.

JULIA: Wait. How did you know we're a "no" house? How do you know which house is ours?

TIM: Um. Ma'am, I'm not paid to stand around talking to you.

JULIA: I'm not paid to talk to you either. In fact, I'm not paid to question this plebiscite at all. Whereas, it seems, you and quite a few of your friends are paid to talk to the good people of Kitimat. Where are you from?

TIM: Edmonton.

JULIA: Are those brochures?

TIM: Yes, ma'am. If I give you one, will you leave me alone?

JULIA: I'm not bothering you, am I?

TIM: A bit, ma'am.

JULIA: I'm not calling you on your time off, am I? Or knocking on your door during your family time, am I?

TIM moves off.

ACT TWO – Scene Twelve

Kitimat, February 2014. CHORISTER 1 (DIRECTOR), CHORISTER 2 (CAMERAPERSON), and NUNO are making a commercial. MARTA enters and watches.

CHORISTER 1 (DIRECTOR): Action!

NUNO: There's no question this is what Kitimat needs. (*out of character*) Wait –

CHORISTER 1 (DIRECTOR): Yes?

NUNO: Does it matter that I work for the smelter and not the pipeline?

CHORISTER 1 (DIRECTOR): No, no. That's not the point. We need a caring, strapping, young worker like yourself. And who knows, you *could* work for the pipeline.

NUNO: I'm not sure if I remember my lines.

CHORISTER 1 (DIRECTOR): That's okay. Do your best. We're still rolling. You can go.

NUNO: (*trying to get back into character*) This is my home. I don't want to have to leave. Now I don't have to. That's why I'm voting "Yes for Kitimat." We need the jobs. Of course I care about safety – it's my life on the line. And the environment – I'm always out in it. Fishing, hunting –

CHORISTER 1 (DIRECTOR): Maybe not with the hunting. It's okay, we'll edit that in post. We're still rolling.

NUNO: I chop wood for my neighbours.

CHORISTER 1 (DIRECTOR): Great! Cut! I'd love some shots of you driving your truck around. In the woods …

NUNO: Awesome.

NUNO runs over to hug MARTA.

ACT TWO – Scene Thirteen

The Viveiros living room, March 2014.

BARB: You knock on the door –

JULIA: Just walk up and knock? Oh, I'm not sure I could do that.

BARB: You'll have someone there, taking notes. With you. It won't be that scary. It's actually kind of fun.

JULIA: Fun? (*laughing*) Never in a million years would I imagine that.

BARB: People want to talk about it. They can't talk about it at work. Or at the mall. Or with their family. They're scared of losing friends.

JULIA: I'm not sure I have all the facts.

BARB: You will. We'll make sure you will. (*beat*) You look kind of stressed out.

JULIA: I am. All that company is doing. All the money they're spending. You guys need help. There are so many houses and so few of you.

BARB: We do need help. (*pause*) But I don't want you to do something that's wrong for your family.

JULIA: I'm in. God, I'm so nervous. I haven't ever done anything like this. Before, I just took care of my family, answered phones at the real-estate office.

BARB: That's why you'll be good.

JULIA: I hope so.

BARB: It's like David going to fight the giant Goliath. All David had was a little sling and five smooth stones. But David was the right guy for the job. With what he had, with what he could do. And we need what you can do, Julia. We do.

JULIA: Okay.

> *BARB exits. She crosses paths with MARTA. They glare at each other. The CHORUS members as Kitimat residents put up signs reading "Yes for Kitimat" on their lawns and homes.*

ACT TWO – Scene Fourteen

The Viveiros home, March 2014.

MARTA: Julia, I'm no longer asking. I demand that you stop.

JULIA: No.

MARTA: How dare you?

JULIA: Because I have to. I can see why you think like this, Marta; we were brought up in a time when the company took care of us. But that's not what's happening now. Why do these companies think we need them to survive? No matter what they do?

MARTA: We do need them.

JULIA: No, we need air, and water, and soil to survive.

MARTA: I haven't seen anybody taking air and water and soil to the bank, have you?

JULIA: I'm not going to stop. This is who I am now.

MARTA: Oh, please.

JULIA: Why am I the one who's supposed to shut up? Why don't you stop?

MARTA: Because I believe in Kitimat.

JULIA: Maybe places like Kitimat have a life and a death. Like people.

MARTA: We should be able to plan better than that.

JULIA: We should. This house, this sofa, their value – all skyrocketing, right?

MARTA: Yes.

JULIA: But it's my home. It's where I want to live. I don't want to profit off of it. All this is nothing compared to our real home.

MARTA: Our real home? What are you talking about?

JULIA: This planet. Earth.

MARTA: Oh my god. Please. You're becoming a complete hippy radical freak. You've probably gotten yourself on some terrorist surveillance list.

JULIA: What if I have?

MARTA: Next thing I know, you'll be getting arrested.

JULIA: I will if I have to.

Upset, JULIA crosses to the sofa and begins tearing off the plastic cover.

MARTA: What are you doing?

JULIA: It's my house now. And I don't want plastic all over everything.

MARTA: It keeps it nice. Mom and Dad were so careful. It's become collectible. It's worth a lot of money.

JULIA: There's more to life than money.

MARTA: Of course there is. Julia, look at yourself, you've lost it. You have.

JULIA: I want you to leave.

MARTA: But this is my home. My childhood home.

JULIA: If you loved me, you wouldn't be trying to silence me.

MARTA: I love you.

JULIA: I love you. But you can't shut me up. Go!

MARTA is heartbroken. She exits, respecting JULIA's wishes.

ACT TWO – Scene Fifteen

Manny and Julia's bedroom in the Viveiros home, March 2014.
JULIA is kneeling before her statue of Mary. ANA catches her.

ANA: Oh my god.

>ANA *crosses and picks up the statue of Mary.*

ANA: Why are you praying?

JULIA: My mother taught me. I find it comforting.

ANA: A virgin birth. I don't find that comforting at all.

JULIA: (*smiling*) You're funny, Ana.

ANA: What? It's the truth.

JULIA: Sometimes things get so big, beyond us. At one of our meetings, the Chief Councillor for the x̄á'isla Nation, Chief Ellis Ross, came by.

ANA: Whoa.

JULIA: He thanked us. He said, this is your fight, not our fight, but thank you. And then, whoosh, he was gone. It was incredible.

ANA: Did you hear what happened at the basketball game?

>JULIA *shakes her head.*

ANA: There was a flash mob! At the end of the game – it was a nail-biter – the x̄á'isla threw hundreds of No Pipeline shirts into the crowd – and everyone put them on and started chanting "No Pipeline!" and the mayor couldn't finish her talk. It was awesome. Then the mayor said, "You don't mix church and state, and you don't mix recreation and politics."

JULIA: Ha!

ANA: Industry built all our stadiums.

JULIA: I know.

ANA: What's happening to our town? To our family?

JULIA: I don't know. I guess we're deciding what matters. Ana, are you okay?

ANA: I guess.

JULIA: How is it at the pub?

ANA: Good money. Good to have a job.

JULIA: Watch out for those guys at work. Guys don't always –

ANA: What?

JULIA: Think things through. The way you have to if you're a woman.

ANA: Mom, that's bullshit. We can be like the guys.

JULIA: Of course we can. I'm just saying –

ANA: What?

JULIA: We carry babies. It makes us different.

ANA: Duh.

JULIA: I don't like it either, but a man's reputation goes up if he –

ANA: Yeah, and a girl's goes down. I know.

JULIA: Ana, I'm trying. My mother never talked to me about any of this.

ANA: Whoa. I thought in the old country the women were all close. Didn't they see what the animals do? I thought sex ed would be fairly obvious.

JULIA: It was all shrouded in silence and mystery, Ana.

ANA: Okay.

JULIA: I don't know what to say to you.

ANA: Okay.

> *ANA pauses, gives her mom a break, smiles, and puts the statue back.*

ANA: All silence and mystery.

> *JULIA becomes emotional and embraces ANA.*

ANA: Mom, Mom, I got to go to work.

> *ANA exits. Meanwhile, CHORUS members hand out Yes for Kitimat brochures to the audience.*

ACT TWO – Scene Sixteen

The Viveiros living room, March 2014. BARB enters with a Yes for Kitimat brochure.

BARB: I felt a cold chill up my back when I saw these. It's their new ad campaign.

BARB shows JULIA the brochure.

JULIA: Wait. I know her. Isn't that ...?

BARB: Yep.

JULIA: Why did she do this?

BARB: She wants her husband to keep his job. She's taking a lot of flack for it now.

JULIA: Oh my god. Is that ...?

BARB: Yep.

JULIA: They got a whole family? How? And they're dropping off these brochures at every home in Kitimat?

BARB: Not just here. They're running those billboards and ads in newspapers everywhere, in Kitimat, Smithers, Prince Rupert, Terrace, Prince George, Vancouver. They've got paid canvassers, phone pollers, billboards, PR specialists, a colour theme, they got radio, they got TV.

JULIA: And we've got volunteers with little photocopied sheets and homemade, recycled signs going door to door. What chance do we have? There's too many neighbourhoods, too many houses for us to reach.

BARB: Yup.

They both look dejected. MANNY enters.

MANNY: Hello, ladies. Guess what happened to me today.

JULIA: I don't know.

MANNY: My boss calls me into his office. He says, "I've seen your wife on TV."

JULIA: Oh god. Manny, what will we do –

BARB: Maybe I should go.

MANNY: No, no. I thought he was going to lay me off, but wait for it –

JULIA: Okay –

MANNY: He says, "I've seen your wife on TV. And she was great. Standing up to her sister. I loved it."

JULIA: What?

MANNY: He watches all the City Council meetings. He says they make the best reality TV. And he says he wants to donate to your organization.

MANNY hands JULIA some money.

JULIA: (*laughing*) Wow.

MANNY: Julia, I'm getting stopped at the mall, and the bank, and at work. People don't want to talk about it – they don't want to lose friends or family over this – but very quietly, they sidle up to me and say, "Way to go." Way to go, Julia. Way to go, Barb.

ACT TWO – Scene Seventeen

The smelter's dock at Hospital Beach, March 2014. JIMMY is waiting around. ANA storms up. He offers her a smoke, but she shakes her head.

JIMMY: I'll get us a hotel room, baby, if that's what you want.

ANA: They're all booked.

JIMMY: Camp is –

ANA: I don't want to meet you at the work camp. I – I'm freezing.

JIMMY hands her his big coat.

ANA: Now you'll be cold.

JIMMY shakes his head: he doesn't mind.

ANA: Guess what? I'm late. I might be pregnant. I think I am.

JIMMY: Oh, baby, I'm sorry.

ANA: You're sorry?

JIMMY: Aren't you?

ANA: Yeah.

JIMMY: Such a bummer. I'll totally help you with it.

JIMMY reaches in his wallet and hands ANA money.

ANA: I –

JIMMY: I been here before. I'll take you, I'll get off work.

ANA: You mean for an abortion?

JIMMY: Well … yeah.

ANA pauses for a moment, then takes the money.

ANA: Thanks.

JIMMY: Sure.

The CHORUS begin asking members of the audience, "Do you have any reservations about the oil industry?" They then shout out their interviewees' answers for all to hear. Examples: "This woman has no reservations about the oil industry!" or "This man is worried about whales!"

ACT TWO – Scene Eighteen

MOM's Cuisine, a Portuguese restaurant in Kitimat, March 2014. MARTA and ANA are seated at a small café table, having espressos and queijadas de leite (milk tarts).

MARTA: Where do you see yourself in five years?

ANA: It's strange: Grandma, she didn't ever have to –

MARTA: What?

ANA: Do this. Make goals for her life.

MARTA: She didn't have the *opportunity*.

ANA: Yes. It was all mapped out. She was in charge of making a family.

MARTA: Is that what you want?

ANA: What if I did?

MARTA: I'd tell you that most men aren't like your grandpa, or your dad.

ANA: You got that right.

MARTA: I'd tell you to make a plan of your own. You're good with money, management.

ANA: You think so?

MARTA: Of course you are, Ana. Living in that house, it's lowered your confidence. Restricted your horizons.

ANA: I'd like to make more money.

MARTA: That's the spirit. Do you want to get your ticket in something?

ANA: Oh, like Nuno.

MARTA: Women can, you know. But it's a tough life. I think you're incredibly smart. You're curious. You'd love university.

ANA: I'm not sure I want to leave Kitimat.

MARTA: I know, I feel that bond too. But you can go away and come back.

ANA: Are you sorry you did?

MARTA: That I went away or came back?

ANA: Both. Either.

MARTA: I'm not sorry for anything I've done.

ANA: I'm not saying you should be.

MARTA: Ana, I'll pay for you to go to university.

ANA: What? Wow.

MARTA: I believe in education for women. And what could be better than for me to support a woman in my very own family?

ANA: (*hugging MARTA*) Wow.

MARTA: You can start looking at things online. Dreaming.

ANA: Okay. But Auntie Marta –

MARTA: What?

ANA: You talked to Mom about this?

MARTA: No.

ANA: You and Mom, you're fighting, right?

> *MARTA nods.*

ANA: I don't want to be a pawn in whatever's going on between you. But I promise to think about it, okay?

ANA gets up to leave. MARTA gets tears in her eyes, quickly wipes them away, and nods.

ACT TWO – Scene Nineteen

The Viveiros living room, March 2014. CHORISTER 3 as canvasser walks up to the Viveiros door and knocks. MANNY opens.

CHORISTER 3 (CANVASSER): Are you aware what the pipeline will do for Kitimat?

MANNY pulls out a camera and takes a picture of CHORISTER 3 (CANVASSER). They run off.

MANNY: How do you like it!

ANA: Dad, that was awesome.

MANNY: You grow up under fascism, you get some ideas.

ANA: What was it like? The Azores are so remote. I didn't think they were that affected.

MANNY: Salazar squeezed everything from us and gave nothing back. People went hungry growing food for his empire. Informers planted in each village. But you could outwit those guys.

ANA: Guess we're going to have to get smart like that.

MANNY: The Azores, my Ana, are one of the most beautiful places on earth. Houses made of black lava, with red roofs and white walls ... the sea stretching out for thousands of miles. That's where we're from. Some call it Atlantis.

ANA: Wow, Dad.

MANNY: Don't forget where you're from. Promise me. Don't forget who you are.

ANA: I won't. Dad, Auntie Marta thinks I should get out of here. She says she'd help me. Go to university.

MANNY: What do you want?

ANA: I don't know.

MANNY: Ana, an education.... that would be a treasure. To do something for work that doesn't wear out your body. To be able to have the time to think about how things could be. Maybe even to speak out without fear of losing your job. I have some money saved, we can help you go too.

ANA: I don't want to leave you guys.

MANNY: I know, but there's nothing here for you, is there?

ANA: No.

ACT TWO – Scene Twenty

Kitimat, March 2014. JULIA and BARB are going door to door. JULIA is speaking, while BARB is taking notes. CHORISTER 1 as citizen answers the door.

CHORISTER 1: Oh, hello. I'm voting no. Come in, come in. Do you want some cookies, some tea?

JULIA: I can't – if you are voting no, that's great, but we have to move on. We have to go talk to undecided people.

CHORISTER 1: Oh, right. Of course. But wait. I want to give you some money.

CHORISTER 1 grabs their wallet and gives JULIA some money. She stares at it.

CHORISTER 1: You go make an ad.

JULIA: Oh, okay.

BARB: Thank you.

JULIA and BARB go to the next home.

JULIA: Hello. Can I talk to you about the proposed pipeline?

CHORISTER 2: Okay. Wait, I know you. You are the receptionist at the real-estate office.

JULIA nods. She and BARB go to next house.

CHORISTER 3: You watched my daughter when she was little.

Again, JULIA nods. She and BARB go to next house.

CHORISTER 4: I was at chemo with you and your mom.

JULIA: Yes. What are your concerns?

CHORISTER 4: Jobs.

JULIA: Do you know it's only about fifty to sixty permanent jobs?

CHORISTER 4: What? The new Timmie's[20] employs more people than that!

JULIA: Close to it.

JULIA and BARB go to the next house. The CHORUS members gather around them.

CHORISTER 3: I have to be realistic.

JULIA: It's them that aren't being realistic. The science just isn't there.

CHORISTER 3: You know, you're right. I boat in the summers –

JULIA: Yes, I saw the boat in your driveway.

CHORISTER 3: There's no way they could clean up a spill in the winter. It gets all frozen up in there. Sometimes three days at a time.

CHORISTERS 1, 2, 3, and 4 exit. JULIA and BARB go to the next house.

CHORISTER 5: I'd love to vote with my heart. But I've got to use my head.

JULIA: Vote with your heart.

CHORISTER 5: I can't. I'm sorry.

CHORISTER 6 as husband of CHORISTER 5 comes out from the back, wearing only a blanket. He is on the verge of exposing himself. JULIA tries to avert her eyes and keep from laughing.

CHORISTER 6: (aggressively) What are you doing talking to my wife?

JULIA: I'm talking to her about the plebiscite, sir.

CHORISTER 6: (aggressively to CHORISTER 5, his wife) What are you doing talking to her?

CHORISTER 5: (cowering) I'm sorry, honey.

CHORISTER 6: You, get back in the house!

JULIA: Can I give you my flyer?

---

20 Tim Hortons coffeehouse.

CHORISTER 6: Get the hell out of here!!!

CHORISTER 6 begins waving his arms, almost showing his privates or his naked bum.

CHORISTER 6: You people, you're being bought by a bunch of Hollywood celebrities.

JULIA: It's just us, sir. We turned down outside help.

CHORISTER 6: Get out of here, you with your celebrity hippy outside help.

JULIA: I'm from Kitimat, sir.

JULIA backs into a Yes for Kitimat sign on his lawn, as CHORISTER 6 keeps screaming at her. JULIA falls and laughs.

JULIA: He's who I was scared of?

BARB: Who really listens to him?

JULIA and BARB laugh.

BARB: We should make an ad.

JULIA: How? I've never done anything like that.

BARB: None of us have.

The CHORUS enters and enacts the ads that JULIA and BARB's team eventually creates. CHORISTER 1 as director and CHORISTER 5 as cameraperson are filming the ad in which CHORISTERS 2, 3, 4, 6, and, lastly, JULIA are acting.

CHORISTER 1 (DIRECTOR): Action!

CHORISTER 4: As the younger generation, it's our job to protect the land.

CHORISTER 2: I want my children to catch fish from the river.

CHORISTER 3: I don't want them to fear an oil spill. Take care of what we have now.

CHORISTER 6: Protect the future for our children.

JULIA: (*joining the CHORUS and taking part in the ad*) No amount of money can bring back what we're risking.

ACT TWO – Scene Twenty-One

The da Terra living room, 1958. Late 1950s music. CLARA and JOSÉ enter their living room.

CLARA: (*in awe*) Querida, something so wonderful has happened.

JOSÉ: Yes, my love?

CLARA: Our prayers have been answered.

JOSÉ: Oh Clara!

CLARA: Yes. I'm going to have a baby. It's wonderful, wonderful. I can feel this baby's soul. If it's a boy, I'll name it José. A girl, Marta, after my sister. I think it's a girl. I have such dreams for her. She might be able to go to university. And make her way in this new land.

JOSÉ: Oh querida.

CLARA: Kitimat. A strange place to have a baby. The women at the supermarket, they tell me they have no one to show their babies to except each other.

JOSÉ: Forty-two babies born a month.

CLARA: Kitimat. A strange place, José. But we will make it beautiful. For our baby. For Marta.

JOSÉ: For Marta.

JOSÉ and CLARA look out, pouring all their drive and potential into the dream of their daughter.

ACT TWO – Scene Twenty-Two

The smelter's dock at Hospital Beach, March 2014.

NUNO: You're pregnant?

ANA: No, but I thought I was. He gave me money to take care of it.

NUNO: That's cold.

ANA: It's practical.

NUNO: What a sleaze. I'm going to kill that guy.

ANA: He's left town. (*pause*) Saw your ad with the truck.

NUNO: Yeah. Let's not talk about it, okay?

ANA: Sure. (*pause*) Your Kitimat suitcase, twenty-four beers. It's no joke. It's a whole thing. Sometimes the only way to fly out of here is on the wings of sex and alcohol.

NUNO: Yup.

ANA: How did it get to be like this, Nuno? Our people – Portuguese people – I'm not saying we were saints, obviously, but Grandma, she believed in charity, goodness, hard work, making a new life. There is such sweetness here. But when it comes down to it, are we the people that poisoned the river? That changed a way of life that's been here since the beginning of time?

NUNO: We're just the workers. People above us are making the decisions.

ANA: But what about all the people who stand up? In Kitimat, there were all those strikes. That wasn't easy.

NUNO: Yeah, but people are lazy now.

ANA: Maybe. Grandma and Grandpa, they could live off the land and the sea, make their own clothes, garden. We can't do any of that.

NUNO: I'm glad I don't have to do all that stuff. Aren't you?

ANA: I guess.

NUNO: I'm glad to have electricity. Heat. And you don't seriously want to go back to the way things were for women in Grandma's time, do you?

ANA: No. But maybe we could pull the most beautiful threads out of their dreams and make something for our time. Like, don't you ever want to go back? To the Azores?

NUNO: I have, like, no connection to that place.

ANA: It's so weird. Grandpa found a way to put down roots. Now we're back to being temporary workers.

NUNO: What's in the beer tonight? You are totally tripping out.

ANA: Your mom said she'd pay for me to go university. It's got me thinking all these wild thoughts. Nuno, why don't you come with me? Please. I'm sure your mom would help you go, too.

NUNO: Why would I?

ANA: I don't know, to learn stuff.

NUNO: I make twice the starting wage of a college professor.

ANA: What if the work runs out?

NUNO: It won't.

ANA: Are you worried about the vote?

NUNO: No. People aren't going to vote against their own best interests.

ACT TWO – Scene Twenty-Three

The Viveiros home, April 2014.

MANNY: Where are you going to watch the results?

JULIA: We didn't get to all the houses.

MANNY: It was impossible.

JULIA: I'm so nervous.

MANNY: You should go, be with your group.

JULIA: Okay.

MANNY: Wait –

JULIA: Yes?

MANNY: How does it feel? To speak out?

JULIA: It's scary – but –

MANNY: Yes?

JULIA: It feels good. Really good.

> *MANNY smiles. JULIA kisses him, then exits. She re-enters.*

JULIA: I love you. You stand by me when it matters most.

MANNY: Julia, you've found a beautiful way to honour José and Clara's memory. You have. Now go! Find out how everyone voted!

> *MANNY and JULIA exit. In the following section, the CHORUS whispers the results of the vote all around the audience, "yes" or "no." Individual characters step forward from the CHORUS and the main cast to give their votes.*

NUNO: Yes.

MANNY: No.

ANA: No.

BARB: No.

TIM: I can't vote. I don't live here.

JULIA: No.

MARTA: Yes.

> *JULIA crosses back to her house. She embraces MANNY and ANA.*

JULIA: I'm so nervous.

BARB: We all are.

JULIA: What do we do?

BARB: Wait until we hear.

CHORISTER 1: I've just been texted the results.

CHORISTER 2: Read them out!

CHORISTER 1: Forty-two percent voted Yes. Fifty-eight percent voted No!

JULIA: Oh my god, oh my god.

> *A cheer erupts from the crowd. Everyone starts hugging each other. We hear the sound of cars honking.*

JULIA: Why are they honking?

BARB: They're cheering for us. For Kitimat. It doesn't get any more grassroots than this.

> *We hear the sound of distant drumming, moving closer.*

BARB: It's the x̄á'isla. They said they'd be here for us, and they are.

JULIA: I can't even begin to understand the beauty, the symbol of that.

BARB: We're coming together.

> *CHORISTER 4 as reporter addresses JULIA, with CHORISTER 5 as cameraperson rolling the camera.*

CHORISTER 4 (REPORTER): How does it feel?

JULIA: It's one of the most beautiful moments in my life. I've completely changed through this. It's magical. They can't take away this victory. Ever. I feel like ... a citizen.

JULIA sees MARTA. She crosses to her and embraces her.

ACT TWO – Scene Twenty-Four

The Viveiros Home, August 2014. JULIA hands Clara's old suitcase to ANA.

ANA: What's this?

JULIA: Your grandma's suitcase. I thought you could use it.

ANA: (*opening it*) A rosary. A shawl.

ANA puts the shawl on her head. She looks like Clara.

ANA: A photograph of her family.

JULIA: Your family.

ANA: I don't know them.

JULIA: They're still our family. (*referring to the suitcase*) It'll bring you good luck. For going into the unknown. Ana, it's a precious thing. For a woman to get an education. It can take generations.

ANA: It was great, Mom, what you did.

JULIA: The "no" was here, in Kitimat, all along. All we did was help it come out. (*referring to something in the suitcase*) What's that?

ANA: A holy card. (*reading, or attempting to read, the Portuguese text*) Ave Maria, cheia de graça ...[21]

JULIA: It was all my mother had, when she came to this country. A mala da esperança.

ANA: "Mala" is ... suitcase? "Esperança" ... hope?

JULIA: Yes, a mala da esperança.

ANA: (*laughing a little as she realizes*) A Kitimat suitcase.

JULIA: (*turning to the audience and smiling*) There is a Portuguese song, written by the great Amália Rodrigues, our mother used to sing ...

---

21 Hail Mary, full of grace ...

CLARA enters and sings Mariza's "Ó Gente da Minha Terra"
(Oh, people of my land), composed by Tiago Machado (music)
and Amália Rodrigues (lyrics): "É meu e vosso este fado ..."
As CLARA sings, all other cast members enter and stand.

JULIA: (*at the end of "Ó Gente da Minha Terra"*) I used to wonder, "Who are the people of my land?" Now I know it is you. I received my sadness from you, but also my joy. (*to the audience*) Thank you.

The End

ACKNOWLEDGMENTS

for Kitimat

Charles Simard, Kevin and Vicki Williams, Mellon Foundation's Elemental Arts Initiative, Pomona College Department of Theatre, Nancy Nyce, Dr. Onésimo Teotónio de Almeida, Dr. Francisco Fagundes, Diniz Borges, Dr. Manuela Marujo, Dr. Rosa Simas, Dr. Art Horowitz, Dr. James Taylor, Mary Rosier, Janet Hayatshahi, Sherry Linnell, Michele Miner, Young Tseng Wong, Isabel Semler, Playwrights Theatre Centre, Kathleen Flaherty, Heidi Taylor, Jacqueline Goldfinger, Disquiet International, Naomi Telushkin, Ryan Oliveira, Alexandrina Andre, Brendan Bowles, David Diamond, Sylvia and Leo De Sousa, Giovanni Ortega, Patric Caird, Wendel Meldrum, Benjamin Arthur Gutknecht, Kelly Brown, Janice Valdez, Melissa Stephens, Niveria Oliveira, Peter and Aileen Ponter, Robin Rowland, Rose Klukas, Kitimat Wednesday Hiking Club, Kitimat Valley Naturalists, Anna Cabral, Luso Canadian Association, Patricia Lange, Cheryl Brown, Louise Avery, Kitimat Museum and Archives, Zelia Marleau, Alcina Couto, Eden Robinson, Bill Clark, and Juno Ávila-Clark.

APPENDICES

STATEMENTS FROM DIRECTORS ABOUT THE PREMIERE PRODUCTIONS

As a playwright, I am always enormously grateful to the directors of the premiere productions of my plays. As a reader of plays, I appreciate a window into the first time the text came to life in front of an audience. So I have asked the directors of the premieres of the two plays in this book to provide a memory, something to share with (1) readers and (2) subsequent interpreters. I hope you enjoy these beautiful statements from these talented theatre makers as much as I have!

—ELAINE ÁVILA

The Ballad of Ginger Goodwin

Kathleen Weiss (director):

I remember most vividly the journey of the young actors coming to understand the significance of the struggle of their characters to actually create change in the world. As one might expect, initially, they were held by the personal stories and relationships of their characters, but as we worked on the script as a group, they became deeply engaged in the political issues the script raises.

For future interpreters, I would stress that the script does need a balance between the personal and the political. There is in the *Ballad* a beautiful but doomed love story that should not be diminished by the rousing scenes of unrest that drive the forces of change.

Kitimat

Janet Hayatshahi (director):

A memory I have about working on the production at Pomona College's Seaver Theatre in Claremont, California, was how excited the students were to be part of new play development. College students don't typically have the opportunity to see a script move through many iterations in order to find its strongest voice. These students spent time workshopping the play, then rehearsing it with the playwright in the room, knowing that rewrites were part of the process. Draft number twelve was what we were on for the opening of the show – and the students' enthusiasm for this process was palpable.

As with any good story, *Kitimat* is not about just one thing. At its heart, it is a story about family and that deep unattainable longing that can only be described by the famous Portuguese word "saudade" – usually translated in English as "longing," "melancholy," or "nostalgia." But the play is also about politics, climate change, and environmental injustices. What makes *Kitimat* dynamic is its effectiveness in portraying the struggles of a family, while also weaving in more global issues, but without being precious or heavy-handed about any of these elements. Striking the right balance in these components of the story will make the play sing.

Through my exploration, I found so many connections between the small town of Kitimat and my own personal story. As an Iranian immigrant, I know first-hand what it means to a community when decisions are made for them without much consideration for their needs or their voices. I also know what it means to have Big Oil in the driver's seat. I have seen how industry has tormented and ripped apart my people, my country, the bit of earth I first set foot on.

FURTHER READING, LISTENING, AND VIEWING

The Ballad of Ginger Goodwin

Books

Susan Mayse, *Ginger: The Life and Death of Albert Goodwin* (Madeira Park, BC: Harbour Publishing, 2021)

Roger Stonebanks, *Fighting for Dignity: The Ginger Goodwin Story* (Edmonton: Canadian Committee on Labour History / Comité canadien sur l'histoire du travail, 2004)

Al King with Kate Braid, *Red Bait! Struggles of a Mine Mill Local* (n.p.: Kingbird Publications, 1998)

Music

Wayne Horvitz, *Joe Hill: 16 Actions for Orchestra, Voices, and Soloist* (New World Records 80672, 2008), www.newworldrecords.org/products/wayne-horvitz-joe-hill-16-actions-for-orchestra-voices-and-soloist

Rebel Voices, *A Little Look Around* and *Warning: Women at Work* (Reveille Music, 1991 and 1997), www.rebelvoices.com/Wall2~1.htm#ALLA

Online

Rossland Museum and Discovery Centre (Rossland, BC)
"Rossland Miners' Union": www.rosslandmuseum.ca/minersunion

On Ginger Goodwin and labour history

BC Labour Heritage Centre
"Ginger Goodwin": www.labourheritagecentre.ca/ginger-goodwin/
"The Ginger Goodwin General Strike": www.labourheritagecentre.ca/the-ginger-goodwin-general-strike/

British Columbia Teachers' Federation (BCTF) / Fédération des enseignants et enseignantes de la Colombie-Britannique (FECB)
Teaching resources from the Labour History Project, by the group Working People: A History of BC Labour Lessons Plans: www.bctf.ca/classroom -resources/professional-development-teaching-resources-search?keyword =ginger%20goodwin

Kitimat

Book

Domingos Marques and Manuela Marujo, *With Hardened Hands: A Pictorial History of Portuguese Immigration to Canada in the 1950s* (Etobicoke: New Leaf Publications, with the Multicultural History Society of Ontario, 1993)

Azorean music

The Bruma Project with Sara Miguel
brumaproject.wixsite.com/brumaproject11
On Bandcamp: brumaproject2018.bandcamp.com/album/bruma-project

António Zambujo, *Outro Sentido* (Ocarina OCA024, 2007), including the Azorean song "Chamateia"
www.antoniozambujo.com/pt/discografia/outro-sentido-2007

Grupo Folclórico de Fajã de Baixo, self-titled album (DisRego DRL-00.10, 1986), including "Sapateia"
Facebook page: www.facebook.com/GrupoFolcloricodaFajadeBaixo/

Online

The Canadian Centre for Azorean Research and Studies (CCARS), "a collaborative, interdisciplinary venture" by the University of Toronto and York University. See especially the Centre's "Chest of Memories," www.yorku.ca/ccasr/memories.html.

On the Northern Gateway Pipelines Project

Natural Resources Canada / Ressources naturelles Canada, "Northern Gateway Pipelines Project" (January 2021): natural-resources.canada.ca/our-natural-resources/energy-sources-distribution/fossil-fuels/pipelines/energy-pipeline-projects/northern-gateway-pipelines-project/19184

Kitimat Valley Naturalists, *Marine Birds, Mammals, and Kitimat Estuary*, Review of Enbridge Project Documents (December 2011): www.ceaa-acee.gc.ca/050/documents/54521/54521E.pdf

National Energy Board / Office national de l'énergie, *National Energy Board Report: Trans Mountain Expansion Project* (May 2016): iaac-aeic.gc.ca/050/evaluations/document/114562

———, *Considerations: Report of the Joint Review Panel for the Enbridge Northern Gateway Project*, 2 vols. (2013): publications.gc.ca/collections/collection_2014/one-neb/NE23-176-2013-1-eng.pdf and publications.gc.ca/collections/collection_2014/one-neb/NE23-176-2013-2-eng.pdf

Testimony from Kitimat residents

Joint Review Panel for the Enbridge Northern Gateway Project / Commission d'examen conjoint du projet Enbridge Northern Gateway (June 2013): iaac-aeic .gc.ca/050/documents/p21799/90737E.pdf

History of Alcan in Kitimat

Brad Cross, "Modern Living 'Hewn Out of the Unknown Wilderness': Aluminum, City Planning, and Alcan's British Columbian Industrial Town of Kitimat in the 1950s," *Urban History Review / Revue d'histoire urbaine* 45, no. 1 (Fall 2016): 7–17, doi.org/10.7202/1042292ar

Kitimat Museum and Archives (Kitimat, BC)
"Search Our Collections": collections.kitimatmuseum.ca

Short films

Prelude to Kitimat (Lew Parry Film Productions, 1953), youtu.be /XB8T7v78Xwo

*This Is Not an Enbridge Animation (Shortt and Epic Productions, 2012), vimeo.com/47788521

"The Kitimat Aluminium Smelter" (Rio Tinto BC Works, 2018), youtu.be /YtOkVSKzshc

"1957/58: The Early Years; Life in a Northern Coastal Town, Kitimat, BC – Part 2" (CanadaMotorSports / Reel Life, 2022), youtu.be/OTeXIzYJhUQ

On the news

CBC, "Kitimat Votes on Enbridge Proposal" (2014): www.cbc.ca/player /play/2448615868

Vancouver Observer, "Kitimat No Enbridge Victory – Vancouver Observer – Mychaylo Prystupa" (2014): youtu.be/t87GL54TQZ8

ELAINE ÁVILA's plays are produced in Central and Latin America, the Azores, Europe, the US, Canada, and Australia. She was awarded Best New Play prizes for *Jane Austen, Action Figure* (Festival de los Cocos, Panamá City), *Lieutenant Nun* (Victoria Critics Circle), and *Café a Brasileira* (Disquiet International Literary Program in Lisbon). Her most recent play, *Fado: The Saddest Music in the World*, won multiple awards, including Favourite Musical and the JAYMAC Outstanding Production from the Greater Victoria Regional Awards.

Ávila has served as the playwright-in-residence at Pomona College in Los Angeles, Quest University Canada, and Western Washington University; as the Robert Hartung Endowed Chair and Head of the M.F.A. Program in Dramatic Writing at the University of New Mexico; and as founder of the LEAP Playwriting Program at the Arts Club Theatre in Vancouver.

She has taught in universities from Portugal to lutruwita (Tasmania), China to Panamá; was the 2019 Fulbright Scholar at the University of the Azores; and co-founded with Caridad Svich and Chantal Bilodeau the International Climate Change Theatre Action, now in its fourth iteration, involving forty-five thousand participants worldwide.

Ávila is currently on the Creative Writing Faculty at Douglas College and lives on the unceded, Traditional, and Ancestral Lands of the qiqéyt (Qayqayt) First Nation and other Coast Salish Peoples (New Westminster, British Columbia) with her musician-teacher husband and their nineteen-year-old, a climate activist and artist.